THE KENSINGTON TEMPLE STORY

JACK HYWEL-DAVIES has enjoyed a distinguished career as pastor, writer and broadcaster. As an Elim minister he was Elim's National Youth Director. His many inter-church activities included Administrative Secretary of the Evangelical Alliance, Director General of the Martin Luther King Foundation, BBC producer and broadcaster, and founder of Coverdale House Publishers and Kingsway Publications. He anglicised and published *The Living Bible*, and is author of the popular biography Smith Wigglesworth *Baptised by Fire*. He currently presents a daily broadcast on London's Premier Radio. Jack and his wife, Joan, live in the village of Whyteleafe, Surrey.

The
Kensington Temple
Story

JACK HYWEL-DAVIES

MONARCH
BOOKS

First published 1998 by Monarch Books

ISBN 1 85424 403 5

Editorial Office: Monarch Books
Broadway House, The Broadway, Crowborough
East Sussex, TN6 1HQ

Scripture quotations are taken from the
King James Version (Authorised Version) of the Bible;
the New King James Version copyright © 1979, 1980, 1982
Thomas Nelson Inc; and the New Living Translation
copyright © 1996 Tyndale House Publishers Inc.

British Library Cataloguing Data
A catalogue record for this book is available
from the British Library.

Designed and produced for the publishers by
Bookprint Creative Services
P.O. Box 827, BN21 3YJ, England.
Printed in Great Britain.

DEO GLORIA

CONTENTS

ACKNOWLEDGEMENTS

Without the support of Joan, my wife, and the co-operation of the host of people mentioned in these pages, this book would not have seen the light of day. And then how can it be possible to have the manuscript translated into an attractively produced volume, and made available to the public without the skills and confidence of a publisher? That man is Tony Collins.

However, my greatest indebtedness must be to Julia Fisher.

One of the verses from the Psalms that has become more relevant to me as I have grown older is in Psalm 37. David said, 'I have been young but now am old, yet have I not seen the righteous forsaken, nor his seed begging bread.' So I would like to take the liberty of turning those words to express my appreciation of Julia. I have been young but now am old yet have I not found so willing and hard working a friend as Julia. In the writing of this book she has always been beside me in both the valley and mountain-top experiences. Writing a book, as opposed to magazine articles, can be a very lonely experience; something I warn aspiring writers in my lectures.

Then, of course, with every good woman there must be a good man. In Julia's case, that man is her husband, Norman. He has willingly sacrificed long periods of their time together to enable her to work with me on this book.

Julia has painstakingly researched the events portrayed in this book. She has also interviewed scores of people, teasing out of them fascinating stories in her own inimitable style. Then she has transcribed the recordings before passing them on to me (all at her own expense), so that I could fashion them into an interesting story.

I thank all my helpers in the writing of this exciting story of KT so that we can all join in giving praise to God for what he has done, and is still doing, at Kensington Temple and now The London City Church.

And that is why I have written this book.

PREFACE

'The last thing that we discover in writing a book, is to know what to put at the beginning,' said Blaise Pascal, the French religious philosopher. So it was reassuring for me to discover that at the beginning of this book are just two words, *Deo gloria*—'glory to God'. I did not want this book to heap praise for KT's success on any one man or woman. The longer I live the more strongly I believe that I am nothing and that *he* is everything.

As I look back on my days at Kensington Temple it is with a deep feeling of gratitude to God for allowing me to be part of its expansion. It has been a truly humbling experience. You will discover that when you read these pages and see how God had to put me on my back so that my face would face him. He required me to give him my complete attention, and then stop talking and start listening. In order for God to use me, he had to break me. It is God who provided the blessings we enjoyed at KT; our part as both pastors and people was to allow him to craft us into suitable vessels to become his channels.

Everything in this book has been written to the glory of

God and it would be serious folly for any of us to claim otherwise.

As well as writing a story for God's glory, what else do I want from this book? I want it to be a source of inspiration and encouragement to all those with a passion for the extension of God's kingdom. This was my aim when I asked Jack Hywel-Davies to write the book.

Yes, it has been a long time in the making. There have been many abortive attempts over the past few years. Perhaps this should not surprise us because it has been evident that Satan had a hand in attempting to thwart our plans. But he did not succeed. And in a way I believe the book has been improved in its many 'rewrites'.

1998 is the 158th anniversary of the laying of the foundation stone of Horbury Chapel, now Kensington Temple, and 1999 is the anniversary of its opening. Today we see some of the results of the prayers of those early-day Christians. But as we approach the new millennium we do so with an even greater expectancy.

I thank God for the part he permitted me to play in the growth and influence of this great church.

Wynne Lewis
General Superintendent
Elim Pentecostal Churches
April 1998

FOREWORD

In *The Kensington Temple Story*, Jack Hywel-Davies has not set out to write history. The emphasis is not on factual detail or meticulous chronology. Rather his chosen style is intimate and personal. Jack has the rare literary ability to draw anecdotal sketches and, by adding a splash of colour to the canvas, present an appealing impression for all to see. He brings together strands from his casual conversations with Kensington Temple people down through the years and weaves them into his own personal perspective. He offers us a series of intriguing and inspiring stories rather than a dry, factual account. And the result is pleasing. It is a delightful cameo, a tantalising taste of Kensington Temple.

In 1991 I had the privilege of being invited by the elders of Kensington Temple to become its senior pastor. My own association with the church by then had already spanned almost twenty years and I was keenly conscious of the rich Pentecostal tradition into which I had been called. The twentieth century has undoubtedly been a 'pentecostal' century. What began in 1906 with a few believers in a converted cattle shed in Azusa Street, Los Angeles, California soon spread to all the earth. Since that day there has been a continuous pentecostal revival somewhere in the world.

According to the missiologist David B. Barrett, pentecostal values and practices exercise a determining influence over almost thirty per cent of current world Christianity. And its indirect influences are almost certainly even wider than that. *The Kensington Temple Story* is but one example of this twentieth-century phenomenon. It demonstrates that the need and hunger for a vital spirituality is as present in Britain and Europe as it is in other parts of the world which are more commonly associated with modern pentecostalism. Personally, I am convinced that God has raised up the Pentecostal movement as a prophetic pointer for the Church of the twenty-first century. It is a salutary reminder that we are nothing without an experience of the power and presence of the Spirit.

Despite this, many modern Christians dismiss Pentecostals as an irrelevant or marginalised minority. There are cultural and historical reasons for that but *The Kensington Temple Story* will help dispel them. For Pentecostals this book is a reminder that the key to our destiny is found in our history. And for those charismatic Christians who are formally outside the Pentecostal movement but enjoy its essentially non-sectarian blessings, it is an invitation to discover their roots.

When you read *The Kensington Temple Story* you will be struck by the recurring themes found in it. God is a multi-generational God. He called Abraham, Isaac and Jacob. So, in Notting Hill Gate, each successive generation has played its part in the purpose of God.

The present features of the church's life were evident from the very beginning. The church was built in Victorian times and named Horbury Chapel. It was led by an 'earnest and thoughful' minister who had a strong missionary and evangelical emphasis. The Congregational believers were known for their zeal in evangelism and their social concern. It began as a church plant from a nearby congregation. All these features flourish in the Kensington Temple of today.

The George Jeffreys era, however, added a further miraculous dimension. The supernatural healings that took place then were so startling that they were reported on the front pages of London's newspapers! And so it is today. Signs, wonders and miracles are a regular part of the ministry. It is happening both in Britain and abroad where the Kensington Temple teams regularly report miracles of healing. The blind are seeing, the deaf are hearing and the lame are leaping!

The present church is most directly related to the tiny Elim congregation that took up residence during the mid-sixties in the building renamed Kensington Temple. It began with a time of foundation in the seventies, experienced expansion in the eighties, and now the work is exploding around the world. With over 500' churches, fellowships and ministries based in Kensington Temple London City Church, the influence is now felt in over 100 nations across the globe. To God be the glory!

As we all set our face towards the new century and the urgent needs of our times, *The Kensington Temple Story* is an encouragement to us. Over the last three decades Kensington Temple has stood at the forefront of church growth and spiritual renewal. It is a testimony to the fact that Christ is alive and relevant today. He is touching and transforming lives. He is healing people's bodies and filling them with power for living. He is the Saviour of all who believe.

Colin Dye
Senior Pastor
Kensington Temple
January 1998

INTRODUCTION

When I was invited to write the story of Kensington Temple I felt very much like my friend Eldin Corsie when Elim headquarters invited him to take his small congregation to Kensington Temple. I was excited at the prospect, but somewhat overawed. I made numerous attempts at first. Should it be anonymous? Perhaps I should approach it as an independent reporter. As a matter of fact, one of my early editors was quite adamant that I should make it impersonal. But it all seemed to be so unnatural to me, and as a publisher of many years I knew that this detached approach would not make a 'good read'. Then my friend Julia Fisher encouraged me to make it a personal story. She was aware that I had known Kensington Temple for more than sixty years, and that I had been closely involved in its life for thirty of those years. In fact, I was with Eldin Corsie when he walked into Kensington Temple in the month of May 1965. Soon the die was cast. I embarked on my personal story of Kensington Temple.

One of the problems of writing a story which touches

many lives is to know who to include and who you are compelled to leave out, just because there is insufficient space. Many of them have become personal and much valued friends since our lives met at KT, and to fail to include them seemed to be like leaving out parts of myself. So I must make it very clear that their absence from these pages should not be interpreted to mean that their contribution to KT's success is less than that of those mentioned. They include such stalwarts as elders Jack Twydell and Len Rodgers. Then there was the tireless work of the late Len Rammell. Some of the former associate ministers, who assisted both Wynne Lewis and Colin Dye, left to take other important responsibilities in Elim such as Dr William Atkinson, now Principal of Regents Park College, and Christopher Cartwright, now senior pastor of Cardiff City Temple. Then there was John Evans who travelled across London every weekend to produce magnificent tunes on the Hammond organ. The list is endless. So to those not mentioned, please forgive me. To include you all would need a second volume.

I have done everything possible to ensure the accuracy of the events covered in these pages. My very good friends and ministerial colleagues Eldin, Wynne and Colin have also read the manuscript, and although I do not hold them responsible for its contents, I am heavily indebted to them for their comments and advice.

Johann Sebastian Bach always inscribed his manuscripts, whether the music was sacred or secular, with the Latin words 'Deo gloria'—'Glory to God'. As I have been writing of the marvellous works God has performed through his servants in Kensington Temple, I can think of no better dedication for this book than Bach's.

The
Background

One sunny Sunday morning in 1985 I decided to take my wife and her friend to Kensington Temple for the morning service.

My first visit to KT had been twenty years earlier. Eldin Corsie was its pastor at the time. I was then one of the executive secretaries at the Evangelical Alliance. Eldin had agreed to take his small band of believers, some fifty or more, from a back-street mission hall in nearby Holland Park to a neglected empty building in Notting Hill Gate called Kensington Temple. Eldin and I had worked together as evangelists in the years immediately after World War 2. But here I was in 1965 with no church responsibilities. Eldin, being aware of this, asked me to assist him face this mountainous challenge in this almost empty church building. So I agreed.

We were an insignificant group. No one noticed the members of our tiny congregation as they climbed the entrance steps of this impressive building with its imposing twin towers. At our first service in the newly cleaned building—the members did a Herculean job—I well remember standing alongside Eldin in that high Victorian pulpit looking down on this small group. We were swallowed up in a galleried building capable of seating almost a thousand. I wondered what would become of us.

Now some twenty years later I was back in Kensington Temple.

Five years earlier, in 1980, there had been a change of leaders. Eldin Corsie left to become principal of a theological college, and a fiery Welshman called Wynne Lewis had replaced him as KT's pastor. You would have to search high and low to find such contrasting personalities. I had heard that things were different at KT, and this did not surprise me having known Wynne since he entered the Elim ministry as a young man. But I hadn't bargained for such a difference! Arriving at KT that Sunday morning in the mideighties we threaded our way through the crowded foyer. The first surprise. There was no room on the ground floor. So the ushers directed us to the balcony. The building was crammed full. We couldn't find a single seat, and the service hadn't even started. Two young people took pity on my wife and her friend and vacated their seats, but I had to make do with squatting on the balcony stairs.

What on earth has happened to KT? I said to myself. When I left the church some fifteen years earlier I had a comfortable seat in the newly furnished pulpit, and about 300 were in the congregation.

But here I was wedged between hundreds of people, breaking London's fire regulations, seated on the stairs of the rising terraces in the balcony. And what a meeting it was. I forgot the soreness of my bottom (until I stood to leave)! The atmosphere was electric, and the noise of the singing almost deafening. And crowds, *crowds* of people were forsaking their scepticism and taking bold steps of faith to become enthusiastic Christians. Sportsmen like the internationally famous cricketer Alan Knott. Garth Crooks, Tottenham Hotspur's cup-tie goal scorer. Night-club and

TV entertainers like Carrie and David Grant. Ex-drug dealers and rising stage stars, students and professors, nurses and doctors, chambermaids and foreign embassy officials, smiling secretaries and their bosses; they were all there. The sea of faces around me were mostly young. By their dress the congregation seemed as if all the nations of the world had sent their children to KT. Filipinos, Chinese, Indians, Latin Americans, Arabs and Jews, as well as Africans from Ghana, Nigeria, Benin, Kenya, Uganda (one had been a cabinet minister in President Amin's cabinet and had miraculously escaped his clutches after her husband was murdered). I later discovered that there were well over 100 nationalities in the congregation that morning.

Even the press came. And some stayed!

One was Geraldine Buckley, a feature writer for a popular glossy magazine.

'How can I get to you?' she asked KT's spritely-voiced receptionist. 'Just take the tube to Notting Hill Gate station, and follow the crowd!' was the reply.

And what a crowd!

Emerging from the underground she discovered groups of laughing, happy people winding their way towards Kensington Park Road. She followed. In her report she described being carried along by a sea of joyful people through the crowded foyer into the main church, there to be greeted by smartly dressed ushers with their distinctive sashes. The place was bubbling with a happy sense of anticipation. A far cry from the painfully 'reverential' atmosphere this sceptical reporter expected to find.

Another striking observation for Geraldine was that there appeared to be no class or colour barriers. A silk-clad, middle-class English matron was chatting enthusiastically with an animated group of Ugandan women, resplendent in vibrant colours. She saw a Rastafarian drummer in serious conversation with a soberly-suited 'city gent'.

'The preaching was dynamic and humorous,' said her report. 'The singing incredible, the atmosphere filled with a powerful magic, and when I left at the end of a long service I felt so happy I could have turned cart-wheels as I walked through nearby Portobello market.'

The sequel to this visit was that Geraldine, who was heavily involved in Buddhism and the New Age movement, became a Christian.

Yes, I could see that KT had changed. Not just because it was full. I was struck by the air of eagerness and expectancy. Anything can happen here, I thought. This church is on the verge of something big, way beyond our fantasies or dreams. But what had happened?

Prayer, of course, has played a vital part in the history, not just of KT, but of its predecessor, Horbury Chapel. All three of KT's senior pastors will be quick to testify to the importance of the prayer support their congregations have given them. For example, a team of Africans led by an ex-army major from Ghana and an African princess from Uganda, gave themselves to fasting and praying for three days and nights each week for months on end. This prayer support continues in the thousand-strong praying 'watchmen' of today.

There are three principal leaders in my story of Kensington Temple: Eldin Corsie, Wynne Lewis and Colin Dye. They all make an indispensable contribution to its success. Although they are different personalities, they all subscribe to the same vision for KT, and from my privileged viewpoint I can see a remarkable harmonisation of their God-given gifts and talents. In fact, I would go so far as to claim that in addition to the contributions they made to KT's success the timing and order of their arrival at KT was far from accidental.

The beginning

One hundred and fifty years ago a group of men and women, members of Kensington's Congregational church in Hornton Street, began to pray for the 'poor and neglected people of Notting Hill Vale', according to the church secretary's minute-book. In those early days Notting Hill was a small village on the western end of London which, even in those days, 'had its hovels and iniquitous dens of evil'. Charles Dickens described it as 'a plague spot, scarcely equalled for its insalubrity by any other in London'. And I wonder what was in G.K. Chesterton's mind when he wrote, 'There has never been anything in the world absolutely like Notting Hill. There will never be anything quite like it to the crack of doom.'

Dr Kenneth Taylor, of *Living Bible* fame, on a visit to London was asked, 'What part of London would you expect Jesus to visit first if he were to return to Britain today?' 'Notting Hill Gate,' he replied. 'Why?' asked the interviewer. 'Well, that's where all the world seems to meet. I've never seen so many different classes or nationalities in one area in all my world travels.'

But Notting Hill was not forgotten by the 'members of Kensington's Hornton Street Congregational church' who, according to one newspaper report of that time, 'had been deeply moved at a recent prayer meeting and many had wept as they commissioned thirty-seven people who were to pioneer the new work in Notting Hill'. In the notes made by these pioneering Christian men of Hornton Street we read that they, with typical English reserve, wrote that 'additional religious accommodation was desirable' in Notting Hill. But they not only prayed, they put their hands in their pockets. One individual gave £1,000 (I wonder what that would be in today's money?). That was followed by £700 from the congregation. With this money they proceeded to buy a plot of ground on the corner site of the two roads we now call Ladbroke Grove and Kensington Park Road. It cost £630 (probably worth millions of pounds today). On 30 August 1848 a foundation stone was laid, and a year later the completed building named Horbury Chapel was opened. It was so named after the village of Horbury in Yorkshire, birthplace of the Congregational Church's first church treasurer.

Many famous and wealthy Londoners transferred their support from the mother church in Hornton Street to this fledgling church in Notting Hill and brought their servants with them. The frail little English chambermaid, Gladys Aylward, was one. She found Christ in this church when she was a servant girl. And it was in the minister's vestry that she gave her life to Christ. Gladys was the 'missionary-reject', not considered suitable 'material' for missionary service by the many societies to whom she applied. But she was not to be easily thwarted. She went to China unaided and tossed her tiny nose at the sphinxed-face Chinese communists and courageously led hundreds of Chinese children to safety. Her story was made into the Hollywood film *Inn of the Sixth Happiness*.

But the important point to emphasise here is that this church building was born in prayer and possessed a fervent missionary zeal for Kensington and, through the likes of Gladys Aylward, 'the uttermost parts of the earth.' This faithful band of Christians in Kensington's Congregational church regularly met to pray for Notting Hill.

Colin Dye, the present senior pastor, is convinced that Kensington Temple's current success can be traced back to that group of praying Christians in the mid-nineteenth century.

'I believe,' says Colin, 'that Kensington Temple is part of God's covenant with the early Christians in Kensington. When I see us alongside other significant London churches it's very clear to me how and why it works. I think it goes way back to a covenant God made with the Congregationalists in the last century. I'm a great believer in the God of the generations—Abraham, Isaac and Jacob. When Kensington Temple, or Horbury Chapel as it was then called, was built, it was built as part of the covenant God made with those people when they dedicated their work to God. It came from their prayer meetings. From the people weeping; the sacrificial offerings that were taken. God had spoken to them. That was a covenant of his faithfulness and we are still living off the fruit of it today. We don't understand in Europe just how much we're living off God's blessing from former generations. He's blessing the prayers and the faithfulness of former generations.'

I was reminded of the value of such prayers when listening to the testimony of Angie Taylor, a housewife from Surrey, who, in 1997, walked from John O'Groats to Land's End praying for the healing of the broken homes she passed on her long pilgrimage. In one of the visions Angie received prior to her 'walk', she saw a huge stone shelf. This stone represented to her the prayers of the past. 'God spoke to me through that vision,' she said. 'God said, "I'm answering the prayers of ages past."'

I can recognise the similarities between those early days of Horbury Chapel and the Kensington Temple of today: major emphasis on prayer, a vision for the conversion of the unbeliever in and around London, church planting in the satellite programme, and an outreach to the countries of the world.

Not only was Horbury Chapel the result of agonising prayer, but it was the outcome of Kensington's Congregational church's missionary zeal. When a church is missionary-minded you can be sure it will be a growing church. Soon the thirty-seven members grew to 600 and the Sunday school to 200. It even had a weekday school of 300, and these were when day schools were scarce.

Celia Bowring graciously shared with me some of the fascinating stories she unearthed in her research for a novel she is writing. It's based on the Congregational church in Hornton Street, Kensington and the early days of its daughter church, Horbury Chapel. The London Missionary Society, which was the missionary arm of the Congregational Churches, had held its monthly prayer meetings in the church in Hornton Street since 1798. The members were earnest believers who were great prayer warriors. In 1883 a Congregational minister, John Stoughton of the well-known publishers, Hodder and Stoughton, in his book *Congregationalism in the Court Suburb* wrote:

> That at so early a period of this history such a service should be held was an augury for good. It showed that the insignificant band of Christians worshipping in Hornton Street cherished sympathies so large that they swept over the world, and offered prayers that the proclamation of the Gospel might reach the ends of the earth. From the beginning the Kensington church associated itself with the history of missionary trials and missionary success.

John Stoughton again emphasised the importance of evangelism in London as well as far off lands when he preached at the fiftieth anniversary services of the Hornton Street church in 1845. He said:

Every church should be a kind of mission station for its whole vicinity, a centre of exertion and influence telling on the surrounding sphere; a lighthouse built on a rock, lifting aloft the lamps of truth, warning and invitation; or rather a floating light moving in the person of its members through the adjacent district to illuminate the benighted, to guide the wanderer and to save the soul from moral shipwreck.

Today we are seeing these aspirations and prayers answered.

Where is Notting Hill Gate?

Notting Hill is just a couple of miles from Hyde Park in London's West End. To walk the streets of Notting Hill is to travel through 100 countries in a day. It's a veritable reflection of life in many exotic lands. Today KT finds itself at the centre of a bustling kaleidoscope of a 'league' of nations. Here you find the homes of eminent politicians, film stars and members of the aristocracy. But it's also a place of contrasts. Palatial mansions and embassies in 'millionaires' row' stand alongside the cramped bedsits packed into tall terraced houses which once housed the upper middle class.

Sir Peter Parker, former Chairman of British Rail and one time resident of Notting Hill's Bassett Road, writing in the *Evening Standard* not so long ago, said:

You have to have your own good reasons for living here. It's alive and tense with contrasts; rich and poor, black and white, and the spectrum in between; posh antique shops and Portobello Market; starry restaurants such as Leith's, some good bistros and some dodgy dives; bold fringe theatres such as the Gate's, and cool galleries such as Leighton House. There are, it has to be said, the odd spots of real nastiness.

This mixture spreads itself throughout the surrounding district. Nearby are Bayswater's Victorian hotels, regal and elegant in their prime, but now dwarfed by modern tower blocks. Vast, concrete housing estates overlook the remains of period homes that continue to line the leafy squares.

Bruce Fogle and his actress wife, Julia Foster, have a grandstand view of Kensington Temple from the balcony of their home on the opposite side of Ladbroke Road. Bruce, a New Zealander who is no stranger to the scenic splendours of a wide variety of places, had this to say of Notting Hill Gate: 'The Gate is a serendipitous delight. Tranquillity and mayhem. Familiar and strange. Summer is best, if only because we can leave our windows open on Sunday evenings to listen to lilting gospel music from nearby Kensington Temple.'

Now I wonder if Bruce was aware of the significance of that word 'serendipitous'? The noun 'serendipity', which means 'the faculty of making happy and unexpected discoveries by chance', was coined by that distinguished English man of letters, Horace Walpole. In his fairy tale *The Three Princes of Serendip*, he used the word to describe the happy chance encounter he made with Sri Lanka, otherwise known as the 'pearl of the Indian Ocean'. In this story of Kensington Temple I try to describe the experiences of men and women whose paths, by 'happy chance', have taken them to Kensington Temple.

Notting Hill is a cosmopolitan area. It even has its own market—the world-renowned Portobello Market, which is a must for tourists. It's a place where the visiting world and its families browse through mountains of fascinating antiques and a scattering of junk.

And, of course, Notting Hill is world famous for its carnival. This is the time when the exotic colours of the Caribbean flood its streets as the superbly designed floats glide along to the sound of steel bands. When night turns to day for the millions who leave their clocks at home. Kensington Temple's evangelists are not slow to use this event to present the Christian message to the million or so people who throng its streets.

KT is one of the most unusual churches in the British Isles. In fact it is one of the largest and fastest growing. During the past fifteen years it has given 'birth' to more than 100 satellite churches, apart from those in France, Belgium, Norway and Turkey. It has started its own International Bible Institute catering for 300 students, a School of Creative Ministries for the arts, a children's home in Sri Lanka, and the Dovewell Communications Division of the church with a string of publications. There are regular fellowship meetings for lawyers, doctors and nurses, actors and broadcasters, as well as professional sports people. There is also the Oasis Club for the sixties-plus, and clubs for parents and guardians. It has its panel of approved prison visitors, and a whole series of social services for the homeless, alcoholics and drug addicts. The practical work of the church includes career carers, help for the jobless and a counselling ministry for people in all walks of life. Its 'Watchman' programme has a membership of 1,000 who covenant to pray for KT and its ministries, round-the-clock, twenty-four hours a day. It has hired Thames pleasure boats to cruise the stretches of this famous river through London, conducting prayer vigils as they silently glide past such places as the Houses of Parliament. All these and more operate under the overall title 'The London City Church'.

But riding over all these activities is the ministry of prayer, because the leaders have always recognised that you cannot separate spiritual power from prayer. I well remember Colin Dye speaking to his team of workers at a weekly ministerial meeting. He said that if God decided to take away the gifts God has given him and leave him with only one, he would ask for that to be the ministry of prayer. So it is no wonder that prayer figures prominently in the life of Kensington Temple and occupies a major part of its programme.

Two Welshmen come to London

One of the effects of the Great War of 1914–18 was the denuding of the young life of the churches, especially London. Horbury Chapel felt the blow. In the post-war years its congregation sank to an all-time low.

But God had his man on the scene: Cecil Polehill, one of the famous 'Cambridge Seven'. This was a small group of Cambridge University graduates who had sacrificed their glittering careers to become missionaries to China. In his journeys to the mission field Cecil had to pass through Los Angeles. He had heard that it was there that Brother W.J. Seymour, a humble black man had had the same spiritual experience as the first followers of Christ in Jerusalem on the Day of Pentecost. Brother Seymour was in the habit of seeking this filling of the Holy Spirit with some friends in an obscure wooden-barn-like shed in a back street of this 'City of Angels'. And on 9 April, 1906 the fire fell.

Cecil Polehill was told that this was the fulfilment of the promise in Acts 1:8, where our Lord said to his disciples, 'You will receive power, and will tell people about me everywhere' (NLT). Cecil was a zealous soul-winner, so he was eager to receive this power. At a quiet meeting in a private house in Los Angeles he experienced the same baptism in the Spirit as did the early disciples. This made a dramatic difference to his missionary service among the

Chinese and Tibetans. Later, due to family circumstances, he had to return to England and was subsequently appointed President of the newly formed Pentecostal Missionary Union. In fact, he became the financial benefactor who enabled George Jeffreys to undergo his training for the ministry.

World War I came to an end in 1918, and a couple of years later Cecil Polehill was walking along the streets of Notting Hill Gate when he heard God speak to him. He had previously noticed the large and imposing Victorian church, Horbury Chapel, strategically located at the intersection of two busy roads very close to Notting Hill Gate's underground station. Responding to this inspired impulse he started to ask some questions and found that it was poorly attended. So he approached the pastor, Reverend F.W. Pitt, with the suggestion that he organise an evangelistic outreach in this needy area. Mr Pitt readily agreed, and that led to the gifted Welsh evangelist, Stephen Jeffreys, conducting one of his 'Revival and Divine Healing Campaigns' at Horbury Chapel.

It was a huge success. The meetings were powerful. The Holy Spirit was in evidence. And many miraculous healings took place. So much so that crowds descended on Notting Hill as newspaper reports described these spectacular events. Such a tremendous mail followed, streaming in from all parts of the UK, that it needed special secretaries to deal with them. One newspaper described Horbury Chapel as 'Bethesda in the West End'. Bethesda was the place in Jerusalem where people went to be healed (John 5).

Donald Gee, the well-known Pentecostal leader, then a young man, was the pianist for these meetings. From his vantage point on the platform he reported, 'I shall never forget the smile breaking like the morning dawn over the face of a deaf man when he found he could hear a watch tick. Another night the crowd broke into cheers as though they were at a football match when a cripple walked without crutches.' But sadly, although Mr Pitt wanted 'evangelism', he was opposed to miracles taking place in his church, so Stephen was given his marching orders.

But God hadn't finished with Horbury Chapel.

Within a few years its congregations had diminished again to almost zero, and ultimately it was forced to close. Yet again we see that the hand of God remained on this special building. That early band of Congregationalists from the village of Kensington, who had given birth to Horbury Chapel, was not forgotten by God.

Stephen had a brother called George. God had given both Stephen and George spiritual gifts for pioneering evangelism including healings and miracles. They were conducting their crusades throughout the British Isles. Cities and towns were being turned upside down. George rented the world-famous Royal Albert Hall for the Easter celebrations of the Elim Pentecostal Churches, and each year it was packed to capacity. Even Crystal Palace and its spacious grounds was filled with 25,000 people for Elim's Whitsuntide meetings.

E.C.W. Boulton described many of the supernatural events during the ministry of George Jeffreys in his book *Ministry of the Miraculous*. It says:

> Outstanding manifestations of Divine power were witnessed in services held in 1913 in Smitham, Coulsdon just before our leader, George Jeffreys, commenced the Elim work in Ireland . . . When Mr Miles of Coulsdon, in an unconverted state, attended one of Principal Jeffreys' meetings he was suddenly overpowered by the Spirit and lay prostrate on the floor. He was smitten to earth like Saul of old.

Interestingly this was very many years before what is now called 'The Toronto experience'.

Many of George Jeffreys' meetings attracted the largest crowds for religious gatherings of the day. Not only were the campaigns begun without the support of local churches, they took place in spite of strong opposition from the main-line churches. But, as Boulton says in his book, Jeffreys was following in the footsteps of earlier Christian pioneers. Peter and Paul were thrown into prison. The Wesley brothers were banned from the pulpits of their own church and had to preach in fields. On many occasions they were even imprisoned. This was also the experience of the evangelist George Whitefield. Martin Luther was alone in his stand against a corrupt Pope. The founder of the Salvation Army, William Booth, had to battle alone as he announced the power of the Spirit. He founded his Christian Mission in Notting Hill, which later was renamed The Salvation Army.

There is one sole survivor of George Jeffreys' Revival Party, and he lives in Mitcham, Surrey. He is Albert Edsor, who was the Principal's 'Man Friday'. He was the campaign pianist, chauffeur and secretary. Recounting the many miraculous healings that he had witnessed from his seat at the piano on the platform, he told me that it was a rule that they always waited three years after a person was healed before announcing it in print.

George Jeffreys had opened many churches in London but he still lacked a building in its very heart that would serve as a centre for his international ministry. In addition, he needed to provide a spiritual home for the many converts of his London campaigns. He then remembered his brother Stephen's meetings in Notting Hill Gate ten years earlier. After some discreet enquiries he discovered that this magnificent building known as Horbury Chapel was now empty. However, the Congregationalists were not disposed to sell to him as a Pentecostalist. Undaunted, he arranged for an offer to be made through a businessman in Brighton which the Congregationalists unwittingly accepted. Such was the faith of this Welsh visionary that before he conducted a single meeting in the chapel he arranged for the seating capacity to be increased. His two-week 'Revival and Divine Healing Campaign' in 1930 was just as successful as his brother's earlier meetings. Crowds flocked to the meetings in Horbury Chapel, later renamed *Kensington Temple*. It also became known in the national press as 'The Church of the Great Physician'. I wonder if Wynne Lewis ever knew this because he would regularly say to his congregations, 'Kensington Temple is a hospital for damaged lives. So if you're here for the first time and you're hurting, you're in the right place to be healed.'

Was it also prophetic of Principal George Jeffreys to make KT the headquarters of his World Revival Crusade? A large Victorian house next to KT at 1 Kensington Park Road became the London base for his evangelistic programme. It also became a prayer centre where, every day between 11 am and 12 noon, requests for prayer 'from all over the world' were laid out on prayer tables around which the Principal's team knelt in prayer.

This early international vision was surely divinely inspired because as this story unfolds you will see that this was the vision that Wynne Lewis also received from God as he lay on his hospital bed following a road accident. Soon after Colin Dye took on the leadership he had a similar vision, and one of today's 'coincidences' is that KT has again become a centre for a worldwide revival programme sending its evangelistic teams into many parts of Europe, Central Africa, Latin America, and even countries in the Far East.

Many ask for the secret of KT's success. Perhaps one of the secrets lies right here. KT's pastors and people are generous people. They spontaneously give not only for the spiritual needs of London, or even the United Kingdom, but the whole world.

Kensington Temple again in decline

Sadly, those heady days of the 1930s were not to last. Again Great Britain found itself enmeshed in another world war and much of London had to be evacuated. Consequently KT suffered, but what was more tragic for the Elim family was the personal war George Jeffreys fought with his Elim colleagues.

The Elim Churches were centrally controlled, so much so that in my early days in the Elim ministry there was hardly enough room to breathe, especially for those of us with free spirits. Today there is a greater degree of freedom. George Jeffreys had been raised as a Congregationalist, and even commenced a course of studies with a view to becoming a Congregational minister. And so it was that the first form of church government he encountered was in the hands of the local congregation. Rather late in life he attempted to reorganise the Elim Churches into this form of government. But he failed. His colleagues on Elim's executive council were not ready to give up the power they believed God had entrusted to them. The result was that the Principal left Elim to establish a separate denomination. He presumptuously called it 'The Bible Pattern Church', implying that those who had other forms of government were not based on the Bible.

The renowned philosopher and cleric John Donne is remembered, among other things, for the memorable phrase 'No man is an island'. This is surely the case with the story of Kensington Temple. A lesson for all of us to learn is that our actions, however insignificant, cannot be done in isolation—'on an island'. They invariably affect others. So it was that when this one man, George Jeffreys, decided to separate himself from Elim, Kensington Temple was involved. However, whereas several churches also broke away from the Elim movement, the break was not as clear cut with the members of Kensington Temple. Many of the members, with their pastor, Percy Le Tissier, decided not to be part of either Elim or the Bible Pattern fellowship. Instead they established themselves as an independent church which they called 'The West London Christian Fellowship'.

George Jeffreys and two members of his evangelistic party were life-time trustees of the building Kensington Temple. This gave them the right to use the building for their own services, so the West London Christian Fellowship had to find another building where they could conduct their own services. As all this was happening Britain was 'up to its neck' in the Second World War with Germany. Both the 'split' from Elim and the devastation of London had a disastrous effect on KT. On the other hand, the West London Christian Fellowship managed to keep its members together during the war years in spite of its nomadic life as it moved from hall to hall. But the faith of the loyal members was further tested when Pastor Le Tissier collapsed from a heart attack as he was conducting a Sunday morning service. The leaderless 'Fellowship' turned to Elim for a new minister. As a result, Elim headquarters appointed John Lancaster to the pastorate. At the time the Fellowship was meeting in an ornate church in Queensway. But the members were to suffer a further blow when this beautiful building was offered for sale at a figure far beyond their financial resources. The only place available to them was a run-down mission hall in the back streets of nearby Holland Park. As all this was happening the building Kensington Temple became a sad reflection of its illustrious past. The world war had ended and now with an Elim minister, John Lancaster, as its pastor, the 'Fellowship' now meeting in Penzance Street, Holland Park, found life very hard. It seemed that no one had gained from the 'divisions'. But this faithful band courageously continued in prayer.

In the late fifties and early sixties, two of the three trustees of KT died, the latter being Principal George Jeffreys in January 1962.

Within a short time James MacWhirter, the remaining trustee, released the building following a financial agreement with Elim's Executive Council. I liked James, though some thought him flamboyant. When I was in conversation with him on one of his visits to KT, he said something I haven't forgotten. 'Jack,' he said, 'you'll find that there are two kinds of leaders in the Church. There are the "Unite-ers" and there are the "Divide-ers".' The founder of the Methodist Church, John Wesley, had this piece of advice for church leaders when they encountered people with strongly differing opinions: 'If it be, give me thine hand. I do not mean, "Be of my opinion." You need not. I do not expect or desire it. Neither do I mean, "I will be of your opinion." Keep your opinion, and I mine. And that as steadily as ever. Let all opinions alone. On one side and the other. Only "Give me thine hand."'

Did not our Lord say, 'Blessed are the peacemakers'? KT was about to be pastored by one of God's peacemakers.

Eldin
Corsie

One day in 1965 Eldin Corsie, the youthful pastor of the Elim Church in Penzance Street, Holland Park, was in his study when the telephone sounded.

'Eldin,' announced the caller, 'how would you like to take your congregation to Kensington Temple?' The call was from the Executive Council of the Elim Pentecostal Church at its headquarters in Clapham. Eldin didn't know whether to be happy or scared. When we see today's capacity congregations led in vibrant worship by a talented team of pastors, teachers and evangelists supported by an array of gifted musicians, it is hard to imagine what it was like thirty years ago. In those days even the organist had to be borrowed from an Elim Church on the other side of London.

Eldin's parents became Christians through the preaching of Principal George Jeffreys, so evangelism was in his blood almost from birth. 'My parents had no experience of the Christian faith although my father was the son of a Salvation Army officer. But when he was fourteen he ran away from home, put his age up, and joined the Navy during World War 1. When he came back he couldn't get work. My mother was perfectly godless—she had no background in the Christian faith at all. The thirties were hard times and Birmingham, where they lived, was no exception. They were the dark days of the 'Depression'. However, my mother was able to find work and that helped us as a family.

'One day she was coming home from her work when she heard singing coming from a large auditorium. This was Birmingham's famous Bingley Hall, now demolished. She was a very curious lady, so she climbed the steps and asked a man at the door, "Is this a concert?"

'Instead of answering her question he suggested, "Why not come in and see!" But she hesitated, saying, "Well I have a baby to feed, and my husband will be waiting for a meal."

'This was 1930 and I was that baby. It also happened to be the year in which George Jeffreys, who was conducting meetings in this hall, was also in the process of buying Horbury Chapel in Notting Hill, which he renamed Kensington Temple.

'The man at the door of the Bingley Hall must have been a good persuader. He responded, "Well, why not come in for ten minutes?"' She went in and sat down for ten minutes, stayed for another ten minutes and felt so moved by the preaching that she stayed for an hour and a half! Then, at the end of the meeting, she responded to the appeal from the evangelist, went forward, and prayed the "sinner's prayer".

'She persuaded my father to accompany her the next night, and he too became a Christian.

'My parents were among the first Elim converts in the seventeen churches that were opened in the Birmingham area as a result of that Revival and Divine Healing Campaign conducted by George Jeffreys. Because they were poor they committed the little they had to the Lord, and boxes of groceries began to appear on their doorstep, and money was even slipped through the letter-box. There was no National Health Service in those days when my sisters and brother were very small, so they couldn't afford the services of a doctor. However, my parents would call for the elders of the church to pray for our healing, just as it says in James 5:14. So I was brought up to have faith in God for anything.'

Eldin's father wanted him to have a good profession, as he regretted having run away from his home in the Orkney Islands when he was just fourteen. With that in mind he articled Eldin to a firm of Birmingham accountants. These were the days when 'national service' was in force, and although the war had ended Eldin was conscripted into the British Army. His ancestors, on his father's side, were Scottish so he enrolled in the famous Black Watch Corps. However, when it was discovered that he had been articled to a Birmingham firm of accountants, he was transferred to the Royal Army Pay Corps.

'It was during my period in the Army,' continued Eldin, 'that I was challenged to dedicate my life to the Lord. I was in a queue in the NAFFI canteen waiting for a cup of tea when a young man came along the line giving out gospel tracts. He came to me and began to talk about the Christian life. He seemed a nice fellow so I ordered an extra cup of tea for him, and we sat down at the same table. The remarkable thing was that he talked to me as if I was a heathen! He didn't know anything about my background. I wasn't offended, in fact I was so impressed by his clear stand for the Lord that when he invited me to kneel with him in prayer there in the NAFFI, and in front of my mates, I did.'

Eldin eventually found himself in the town of Reading where he met another Elim evangelist, John Woodhead. He was conducting a Revival and Divine Healing

Campaign. John soon discovered that Eldin was an accomplished pianist. It was too good an opportunity for him to miss because he was in need of a campaign pianist. Eldin agreed, but still had more time to serve in Her Majesty's forces, so when John Woodhead held his next campaign, which happened to be in East London, every evening Eldin would slip out of his army uniform into 'civvies' and travel from Reading to join the campaign party in London's East End. That's how Eldin and I first met because I was also in the campaign team as its song leader.

In 1949 Eldin left the Army and entered the Elim Bible College to train for the ministry. Immediately afterwards he was again 'on the road' campaigning with John Woodhead. By this time John had moved on to Burton-on-Trent with the same tent that he used on the site in London's East End. There were many empty spaces in our cities in those days as a result of the destruction by German bombs. However, in Burton-on-Trent the campaign tent was pitched on a derelict site between two of the country's largest breweries. Was God using these contrasting locations to say something to us? An East London bomb site, with its memories of incredible suffering through death and destruction, was the place where over a thousand people found a life in Christ which nothing could destroy. Then there was the site between the breweries, the product of which numerous people used to try to escape the realities of life. From Burton-on-Trent Eldin moved to Newquay where he not only pastored the Elim church in that Cornish seaside town, but also took on the responsibility of Elim's District Youth Commissioner for the West of England.

By this time a very attractive young lady appeared on his horizon. This lady was Vivien, the daughter of an Elim minister, the late James Kennedy. And, as they say, the rest is history. Vivien left one minister's home to become the 'lady of the manse' in another minister's home, and changed her surname to Corsie. In the late fifties they moved house to Kensington when Eldin was appointed Pastor of the Elim Church in Holland Park. The next step was into Kensington Temple!

Eldin Corsie is often asked, 'What were your thoughts when you took over this large building, Kensington Temple, without any financial backing?'

He usually replies with just one word, 'despair'. He really couldn't envisage at that point exactly what he could do in a short time to make it the kind of place where people would want to come and sit. It was also a tremendous financial commitment. In addition to finding many thousands of pounds this small congregation had to find the money to purchase musical instruments. So they took a step of faith and bought a second-hand Hammond organ. Then he found a good organist—John Evans— who was willing to travel from Clapham. The standard of music was good and John had flair. Being a musician himself, Eldin placed music high in his list of priorities for the development of a healthy and inspiring atmosphere in his churches. This soon proved itself to be true when newcomers to the church said they had been first attracted by the lively singing.

Then, as silently as the sun rises, the church began to grow. Within the first year the congregation had more than doubled, and by the end of the decade the regular congregation was in hundreds. One of the Sunday evening features was to hold a 'guest night' when a special speaker would be invited. On one such occasion Cliff Richard (now Sir Cliff) came, and the Temple was filled to capacity twice in a single night.

Discarded crutches in the basement

While the members were cleaning the building they had to crawl under the floor of the main church which was hardly four feet high. There they found relics of the past. There were signboards carrying the words 'Church Full', and numerous crutches, wheelchairs, leg-braces and other medical aids that had been discarded following the campaigns of Stephen and George Jeffreys during their revival meetings in 1920 and 1930. They became a source of inspiration to Eldin. They were reminders of scenes that could happen again. But they were in a heap of rubble. There was little height in the basement. However, after clearing out the rubble at the far end where the ceiling was higher, they found there was enough space for a little office.

'I believe this activity, with our concentrated prayer life engaged by all the members,' said Eldin, 'had its effect on the atmosphere in the church meetings which became little "power-houses". The church began to grow almost immediately. Some of the former members returned. This would be about 1966 and 1967.'

In the small group that occupied KT in those days there were some very fine men. One of the members from the early days of the church was Mr Burke. 'I considered him to be very important to the church because he was the man at the door,' said Eldin.

'First impressions count,' is an old saying, The Sons of Korah who had duties in the temple of Israel probably knew that. They were famous Israelites. They not only formed one of the temple choirs and composed hymns for the temple services which are now in the book of Psalms, but they were also the temple doorkeepers. In Psalm 84 they say, 'I would rather be a doorkeeper in the house of my God, than dwell in the tents of wickedness' (RSV). These men knew the value of a good greeting for the worshippers coming to the temple. It could make the difference between a good or bad contribution to the temple service that day. They placed greater importance on this ministry at the temple gate than any of their other temple duties. People sometimes mistakenly give credit to the platform party for a successful church service and fail to recognise the 'good mood' first created by the 'doorkeepers'.

Mr Burke was always very smartly dressed in a grey suit and tie. He was extremely dignified and very gracious. Eldin once said to me, 'I think Mr Burke persuaded more people over the steps of KT than anybody else. They would come to the church door out of curiosity, or probably hearing the music and enthusiastic singing, would look in. But Mr Burke would quickly move alongside them and talk to them very kindly and lovingly and get them in. I've been around the world and met people who were once at the Temple and they've always asked about Mr Burke. This man loved his work as one of the Lord's doorkeepers. Sometimes we ministers fail to value such people.'

Mr Burke was one of the early members from pre-war days. Even so, when the split came to Elim he felt compelled to join the members who decided to establish an independent church. This group did not want to be involved in the disagreements between George Jeffreys and the Elim Executive Council. 'When we left KT the last time', said Mr Burke, 'I felt a great burden weighing on me. As I came out of the building I had one word in my mind, the old Hebrew word *Ichabod*.' This is the name given to the mother of the child born at the time the sacred Ark of the Lord had been captured by the Philistines, Israel's enemy. 'She named the child Ichabod saying,

"The glory of the Lord is departed from Israel: because the ark of God was taken."' (1 Samuel 4:21, AV).

'As I turned away, I looked back again,' said Mr Burke. Then the Lord gave me this word—"I shall be back"—that was in 1943. I didn't go back to KT until we took it over again in 1965. That memory stayed with me through all those years.'

There have been many prophecies about the rise again of Kensington Temple. Some of these prophecies I've heard given by visiting Christian leaders, but there are two such prophecies worth mentioning here that were made long before the present surge of revival blessing.

In 1946, just after World War 2 had ended, Principal George Jeffreys was visiting Kensington Temple following one of his world travels. He told the people that God had told him that he had not finished with Kensington Temple. He said God had promised that it would rise again.

A few years after the death of the Principal, Elim minister Frank Lavender also had a prophetic word from God about the future of KT. He described his experience to us during the 1997 Elim conference in Bognor.

'In 1968 I was appointed pastor of the Elim Church in Croydon, on the southern edge of London. Early in my ministry I was travelling from Croydon towards the centre of London when God gave me a heavy burden for this huge city. As the bus threaded its way through south London's maze of streets I was fascinated by the sight of rows and rows of houses. There were high-rise apartments, large business premises and famous hospitals. Eventually we were in Parliament Square and as we passed the Houses of Parliament, the seat of the British government, I was deeply stirred in my soul. With this unexpected burden pressing hard on me, I began to feel overwhelmed. I looked at the changing scenes being unfolded before my eyes as if I were watching a film. I thought, how are we going to reach the millions in this enormous city? Soon I found myself talking to the Lord about it. Then I heard him say, "I am going to move London and change the heart of the nation through Kensington Temple."

'You can imagine my surprise because KT was only about 120 in strength at the time. I must confess that I thought it incredible, yet I was sure it was the Lord. In a strange way I had no doubt that it was God who was telling me to pray for KT. It was a conviction that was so strong that it remained with me. In fact, from that time onwards I began to call on everyone I encountered to pray for Kensington Temple, telling them this story.

'So here in the Elim conference and in various churches where I've ministered, even in America, I've talked about KT and asked people to pray for the church. And I truly believe that what we are seeing now is, in part, the fulfilment of what the Lord showed me thirty years ago. But of course, it's still only early days for KT. I think that even more incredible things are going to happen.

'I remember talking to Wynne Lewis about KT after he had taken over the leadership of the church. Wynne said, "Frank, either we've got to get a church that seats 5,000 people or we've got to open branch churches all over London." Well, it seems that both things have been realised. They've got this large building in North Acton in West London which can seat 4,000. And already they have nearly 200 satellite churches. I understand they're opening another five this month. The whole thing is beginning to explode. But I believe there's much more to come. I am sure that the Lord is going to do what he told me back in the sixties.

'Since I've been able to work in close proximity to members of both Houses of Parliament, it has been a continuing conviction that Kensington Temple will have an effective influence at the centre of government. One of the things I want to see is a strong link between Parliament and Kensington Temple, because KT is such a place of prayer. And I believe that if we can get Christians in Parliament, or parliamentarians generally, in some way linked with KT, it will have a powerful spiritual influence in the Palace of Westminster.'

Frank is a moving 'light' in the Houses of Parliament Christian Fellowship which arranges prayer breakfasts where politicians and church leaders meet for prayer and discussion.

All that seemed to be far away for Eldin that first Sunday when the congregation of fifty or so took their places on uncomfortable wooden seats. Eldin, reflecting on those days, said, 'I certainly had some apprehension, though excited, about the prospect of having such a good position for the church. The building seemed so vast for our small congregation.'

The first thing Eldin did was to devise a plan to reach the community. He based this on a talk he had heard at a seminar he had previously attended. The speaker told how he drew a circle around his church and decided to concentrate on contacting every possible opening in that area.

The first step was to determine the catchment area. For some churches this is not difficult, especially if they are located on a housing estate. But the immediate vicinity for KT included Holland Park and Kensington with its foreign embassies and affluent houses sometimes four stories high.

Eldin started to do the same. 'In my analysis of the area around KT I found a lot of colleges, including the London University Colleges and the Royal College of Music. There were also youth clubs, hospitals and nursing homes. So I made a list of all the places where people assembled and wrote to their secretaries and asked if they would give me the opportunity of speaking at their Christian Union meetings.' As time went by he gained valuable contacts, and slowly new people started coming to the church.

Notting Hill also had its four and five-storey houses but they had been converted into bed-sits, that is, single occupancies for each room in the house. This made visits by KT's outreach teams rather difficult. However, the teams were resourceful and by trial and error they overcame these difficulties. I was reminded of this when I attended a reception in one of the village churches in the area where I live. Unexpectedly a man approached me and said, 'I wonder if you remember me?' I confessed that I had no recollection of him. 'My name is John Heard,' he said, 'and I want to tell you that in 1966 when you were at Kensington Temple with Eldin Corsie, I became a Christian. I was a student at the London Polytechnic and had a bed-sit in Kensington Park Road, just opposite KT. One day one of your young people, Phil MacInnes, dropped an invitation leaflet through my letter-box. It was for the Billy Graham film *The Restless Ones*. Ordinarily I would have thrown the leaflet into the waste-paper bin, but I found that the envelope which contained the leaflet was addressed to me personally. I didn't know the writer, and he didn't know me, but he had taken the trouble to use the electoral roll of the borough to address the invitations by name.' John attended the film show, and that night gave his life to Christ. He is now the Director of the Christian organisation Southeast Asian Outreach.

One of Eldin Corsie's decisions may not have been readily accepted in most Elim churches, and would not have met with the approval of Elim headquarters. Although no attempt was made to hide KT's denominational affiliation he decided not to give it undue prominence: very wisely, in my opinion. This was to allow him to warmly welcome newcomers without giving them the impression that his main interest in them was to have them join his church denomination. He wanted to avoid the charge of brainwashing people, especially the young. He was helped in this by the fact that the core of the church had previously existed as an independent church.

Another kind of evangelism

In the summer of 1978 Victor and Maha found Kensington Temple. That was to begin a very special story, because this husband-and-wife team are probably unique in their ministry.

Victor's life began at Lod Airport in Israel, where he was born. This, say his friends, could not be more appropriate because most of his time seems to be spent flying. Although Victor's father was to enter full-time Christian service in Jordan with the Christian Missionary Alliance, Victor showed no inclination to follow him. After university in Amman he began a career as a newscaster with a state radio station in the Middle East. This led to employment with the United Nations and a large American oil company in North Africa as translator. His life appeared to be very successful. In 1974 he entered business on his own account.

In 1976 Victor and Maha moved to Britain in search of a more satisfying life-style. Within a few months he arranged a huge export of merchandise from Britain and became financially independent. However, one quality of life continued to elude him. He was a dissatisfied man. Peace and contentment were strangers to him. 'I had heard about Christ from my father,' Victor told me, 'and from so many other friends, but sin separated me from Christ. I made it in the business world. I had enough money to live on for the rest of my life, and I really wanted to enjoy life. After two years I squandered most of the wealth I had gathered, but my life was empty. I started to seek for the truth.' Then 'serendipity' visited Victor. Man's coincidences become God's opportunities.

Victor and Maha had now set up home in London where they 'had a happy visit from an evangelist friend from Egypt'. It coincided with the visit of another friend, but he was not a Christian. The evangelist began a conversation with the visitor, who happened to be a Muslim, about Christianity. Then, surprisingly because Victor was himself an unbeliever, Victor stepped into the conversation to tell the Muslim friend what Christianity has to say about heaven. Then the Muslim friend shared what Islam has to say about heaven. Surprisingly, Victor found himself boasting about 'our' Christian faith. 'In fact,' said Victor, 'I didn't know what I was talking about, because I hadn't read the Bible for years.' So Victor turned to his evangelist friend and said, 'Where does the Bible talk about heaven?' He told Victor to turn to Revelation 21 and 22. 'As I started to read these chapters about heaven to my Muslim friend, the Holy Spirit convicted me.' He especially felt this when he read how Jesus said, 'I am the Alpha, the Omega. The beginning and the end.' Then he heard himself saying to this man, 'No one can come after Jesus to finish what Jesus had already finished.'

'The Holy Spirit spoke to my heart,' continued Victor. 'He said to me, "Neither can you finish what Jesus has finished. All you need to do is to accept that."' That night Victor surrendered his life to Christ. Very shortly afterwards Victor and Maha found Kensington Temple and quickly felt 'at home'. Right from the beginning they were grounded in the Christian faith. They were there when Eldin moved on and Wynne came in.

Victor and Maha kept an 'open house', and soon developed a ministry that was to take them away on their world travels which I describe later in the book.

'We opened our home straight away,' Victor told me. 'My mother tongue is Arabic, so we invited people from the Arab world to attend weekly meetings in our home.' Knowing Victor and Maha as I do I can add that these meetings were either preceded or followed by the customary Arab hospitality with delicious Middle Eastern food. Many came to Christ as a result of these meetings. They were then faithfully discipled by Victor and Maha before they returned to their home countries. They continued to keep in touch with Victor and Maha, and many of them extended invitations for Victor to visit them. Slowly but surely this increased into a ministry.

Wynne was quick to recognise Victor's value to the leadership of the church and sent John Harris with a warm invitation for Victor to join the eldership. He is now described as KT's elder with a roving mission.

Roman Catholics visit KT

The church was now beginning to earn for itself a high reputation in the metropolis and this team led by Eldin

Corsie became known not only for the customary vitality of a lively Pentecostal church but also for its biblically based ministry. This was especially remarkable at a time when it was not always popular to be known as Pentecostal. This continued throughout the seventies. The international character of the Temple was also beginning to emerge. Overseas visitors and students arriving in London came to KT and were spiritually refreshed. They in turn spread the news among their friends. Even priests of the Roman Catholic Church 'popped' into this oasis. It became a twentieth-century Elim in their 'desert', a true place of spiritual refreshment. The name 'Elim' is taken from Exodus 15:27 where we read that the Israelites, weary and thirsty from their travels, sat in the shade of seventy palm trees and drank from twelve wells of refreshing water. Many and varied are today's travellers' who have found this spiritual oasis at KT.

One Sunday morning when I was responsible for the communion service during Eldin's absence, I took my place at the church entrance shaking hands with members of the congregation as they departed after the service. This particular Sunday I met a man from Switzerland. Having worked in Switzerland myself, I expressed interest in what he was doing there. He told me he was the Roman Catholic priest for the Italian community in Basel. Somewhat taken aback I asked if he was aware that he was in a Pentecostal church, and that the Catholic church was further along the road. I hadn't expected his reply. He said, 'Yes. Jesus is my Lord and Saviour so doesn't that make me your brother?' He had even taken the bread and the wine as it was offered to him by one of our servers during the communion service.

These were the heady days of the charismatic revival in the historic churches worldwide, and KT figured prominently in the news of this fresh outpouring of the Holy Spirit that travelled the world. At that time I was producer of religious programmes for the BBC which meant I encountered many members of the clergy of the mainline churches who had a deep hunger for the Pentecostal blessing. In Dublin I met a Roman Catholic priest who was leader of a weekly charismatic meeting where 300 priests met regularly for prayer for an outpouring of the Holy Spirit. In Kensington Temple Eldin was finding priests from a variety of places, even the Middle East, in the congregation. Many came to him at the end of the services for prayer.

The arrival of Lyndon Bowring

The Principal of the London Bible College, Gilbert Kirby, had been interested in KT for several years and could see that it would be an ideal training ground for some of his students. So it was that he offered Eldin a team of students. And it was in that team that Eldin discovered Lyndon Bowring.

Lyndon was from an Elim church in Wales, so it was no surprise that he quickly felt 'at home', and shortly afterwards became part of the pastoral team. This is how Lyndon described his first impressions: 'Well it was incredible. All the seats were velvet cinema seats, and the space between the rows was wider than any other known church in the UK. It was comfortable and spacious. Non-church people would come in and be gob-smacked, it was so unchurchy! It disarmed people and from the early days it was a place of mission and evangelism particularly on a Sunday evening. There were nurses and medics from about twenty London hospitals, and students from a similar number of colleges. On the steps of the church before the Sunday evening services the young people would conduct an open-air meeting. An open-air meeting in trendy Notting Hill was so unusual an event that it could not help but attract the passers-by. Members of the team would also travel the streets of Notting Hill inviting people to come to the services.'

Many were added to the church by this means. In Lyndon's opinion there was no other church quite like it in London. 'In fact in those days I did not know of any other church in the whole of London where you could be sure of hearing the gospel preached on a Sunday evening followed by an invitation to publicly receive Christ. So that attracted a lot of people to bring non-Christian friends. Then after church there was always tea and coffee available, and that wasn't usually done in those days.'

Lyndon served with the student team during 1971 and 1972 after which he was invited to take a full-time post at KT. He readily accepted the invitation, and said that he considered it a 'real privilege'. He remained for six years.

'Eldin was the man with the vision believing that God would re-establish this church,' says Lyndon, 'because by the late seventies it was the foremost Pentecostal church in the whole of the UK. But the congregation was always "on the move". It was like filling the bath with the plug out because of the transient nature of the population. The turnover was phenomenal. One of my challenges was to get a firm hold of this mobile population to help to ground them in the Christian faith. I really enjoyed every minute of it. Eldin was always emphasising the need to establish these young people in the Scriptures.'

The congregation already comprised both students and people on short assignments to London, so they had no roots, and Lyndon made it his responsibility to shepherd them saying, 'Look you're here for three months or six months or even three years. Why not give yourself to God? Don't let this be a time of regret and backsliding.'

Kensington Temple is adjacent to the old Notting Hill Gate, so a concerted outreach programme was commenced to reach young people in Notting Dale which is the next district (it's where all the race riots occurred). In this district the internationally famous Caribbean carnival is held every year. A lot of young people eventually came from that district—completely unchurched. So KT gave them everything one would have in a Christian club, then at the end of the evening they were obliged to stay to listen to a ten-minute gospel talk. Today many of the young people contacted in this way have become Christians and are now in full-time Christian service as ministers and some are missionaries abroad. The local borough council considered this work to be of such value to the borough of Chelsea and Kensington that they decided to pay the salary of a youth leader who was employed full time.

The outcome of this outreach was a Friday night-Saturday morning coffee bar when teams of KT members scoured the streets of this very needy, and sometimes dangerous, area late at night, even into the early hours of the morning. During these excursions contacts were made with people leaving night-clubs. Many homeless people were also encountered who were willing to visit the warm and welcoming atmosphere of the Gate Club.

One of Eldin's special gifts was the ability to spot potential talent. Notting Hill Gate had, and still has, an unequalled reputation as a haven for drug addicts and many of them began to look to KT for help. So it soon became evident that KT was in need of a specialist in this field. It was then that Eldin spotted John Harris. John was not only highly qualified in this work, but he also had three Christian rehabilitation centres under his control.

By this time Eldin was beginning to develop a team ministry which included Lyndon and John. They were of great value in helping the many students from various nations such as Sierra Leone, Sri Lanka, Malaya, Singapore, Hong Kong—the list is endless. KT's strategic location was a window of opportunity in those days. People used to say that joining KT one always felt both on the crest of a wave and on the crest of opportunity. It was like a twentieth-century centre for world missions.

Eldin's visits to local educational and medical establishments not only led to an increase in the number of young people joining KT but often resulted in romantic spin-offs. In 1970 Eldin visited the Froebel Institute of Education. In the group of students that subsequently came to KT was a young woman called Celia Bartholomew. That led to her making a personal commitment to accept Jesus as her Saviour. Today that young woman is better known as the wife of Lyndon Bowring.

Lyndon remained on the KT pastoral team for a few years and then moved into other posts until his appointment as chairman of CARE.

By this time it was not unusual to find diplomats, several of high rank, in the congregation. They came hungry and left refreshed, afterwards writing to Eldin to say how they had been able to put to good use the teaching they had received for Christian work in their home countries. Of course, the problem of maintaining continuity in the teaching programmes meant that Eldin and his pastoral team had to adapt to the fluctuations in the congregations. It had, of course, its brighter side. Many of these former students now occupy eminent and influential positions in government and business life. So KT began to develop a kind of movement—a kind of mobile congregation!

'Men and women of influence in all walks of life began

to join us,' says Eldin Corsie. 'There was a businessman, Ian Doulton, who was very successful in the City of London—he used to come with his wife and family. And the Marquess of Reading. He was actively involved in a drug rehabilitation programme and it was not unusual for us to see him surrounded by the recovering addicts he was helping to make a fresh start in life.'

Another pillar of KT during these early formative years was John O'Brien who now occupies the important government appointment of Franchising Director of OPRAF (Office of the Passenger Rail Franchising). He served as honourary treasurer and during the high costs of the building programme was invaluable with his expertise in finance and general management. Even so there was nothing too demeaning for him. Several years later one amusing incident occurred when Delia Smith came as a guest speaker on St David's Day at the invitation of Wynne Lewis. John discovered that the church kitchen, which Delia needed to use for the evening programme, was in a deplorable state. He stripped the kitchen and completely refurbished it in a couple of days, and the famous TV cook had no idea that such a distinguished person had performed a culinary miracle! But John O'Brien was not without his reward, because KT also provided him with a wife!

Another famous personality to enter the doors of KT was the England cricketer Alan Knott. For the benefit of those not around' in the seventies, or who may be not familiar with the peculiarities of England's favourite pastime, I should mention that Alan Knott was a Kent County cricketer from the sixties to the eighties. Recently a computer was used to select the perfect England cricket team of all time. They were Jim Laker, Alec Bedser, Geoff Boycott, Colin Cowdery, Len Hutton, Trevor Bailey, Peter May, Dennis Compton, Fred Truman and Alan Knott.

These were the illustrious England cricketers who were the heroes of every school-boy. To many cricketing enthusiasts Alan Knott is one of the best, if not the best, England wicket-keeper of all time. In his 95 Test matches he was responsible for 269 wicket-keeping dismissals comprising 250 catches behind wicket and 19 stumpings. He was also no mean batsman having scored 5 Test centuries, and a further 30 half-centuries, in a total of well over 4,000 runs in 95 Tests.

Eldin gave us this account of how Alan Knott and his wife, Jan, made their public confession of faith in Christ at KT.

'Alan and Jan gave their lives to Christ in KT in 1973. That was a wonderful experience for me, I shall never forget it. It so happened that earlier in the year we had a visit from a choir in California. Their main feature was a performance of *Come Together*, a musical. They had rave reviews in the States, so we were glad to have them at KT. The evangelist who travelled with them was a man called Bill Severn. Unusually for an American, Bill's father was crazy about cricket, and no mean cricketer himself, which brought him into contact with Alan. So when Bill arrived in London he phoned Alan and this led to a series of events which ultimately brought both Alan and Jan to KT for a Sunday service.

'Lyndon Bowring, who was my assistant at the time, preached that night. Before I brought the meeting to a close I gave an invitation for those who wished to follow Christ to come to the front of the church. You can imagine my delight when Alan and Jan rose from their seats and walked down one of the aisles to the foot of the platform. Then, to my further astonishment as they came forward, I noticed a tramp from the embankment coming down the other aisle. The three arrived before me at the same time. As I looked down from the platform on these two men from opposite ends of society I thought, "This is indeed what KT is all about."

'I was so moved that I felt compelled to descend from the platform and stand with them in front of the congregation. Then, quite spontaneously, I put my hands on the shoulders of both Alan and the tramp. This was, indeed, a testimony to the grace of God. Here was Alan Knott, a world-renowned sportsman and a household name in Britain, who could well be the talking point at the breakfast table of thousands of British homes during the coming week, making his public confession of faith alongside an unknown tramp from London's embankment. Here they stood in full public view before the Communion table on equal terms before God. It was a very emotional experience that day, for both Lyndon and myself.

'And the story didn't end there. After the service Alan and his wife came into my vestry for a chat. In the course of our conversation I asked them if they had any particular problem which they would like to share with me. They hesitated a little, and then Jan quietly said, "Yes, we do have one very private matter. We've been married for eight years and we've been told we can't have children." So I said, "Let me pray for you." They nodded their agreement, and I then knelt between them and asked Jesus to work a miracle and grant them their desire. They thanked me, and left for home. You can imagine my delight when shortly afterwards Alan phoned to say that Jan was pregnant.'

In the mid-seventies, KT had arrived at a position where Eldin needed to share responsibility as widely as possible. So he appointed twelve elders. Each of the elders had an area of responsibility in the church and this took a tremendous load from the shoulders of the pastor. This was the beginning of what KT now calls its 'satellite churches'. 'I became convinced from my experience at KT and from similarly large churches I've visited in the United States, Latin America and Asia that in order to avoid people feeling lost in a large crowd the church should form cells or satellites with an elder to oversee them. This ensures that people have pastoral care on hand.'

Eldin always had a wider interest than just the local church. The word 'ecumenical' is hardly the word to use but he always tried to be in fellowship with other denominations. So as KT came to the notice of political and church leaders he was soon involved in the pioneering projects that endeavoured to clean up the seamy side of London and its environs. He was invited to be one of the first members of the Festival of Light and subsequently served on its executive council. Not only did this affect Eldin, but Lyndon frequently deputised for him and this led to him becoming chairman of CARE, which was the outcome of the Festival of Light. Later on Eldin was invited to join the Council of the Evangelical Alliance and subsequently became its chairman.

KT's evangelistic projects were not confined to Notting Hill. The teams had a stand at Speakers' Corner in Hyde Park. This was good training for the young people as well as a significant witness to the crowds who assembled, mainly out of curiosity and from a variety of countries.

There were also occasions when the notorious area of Soho was 'invaded' by our evangelistic teams, with many unexpected results. This district has an unenviable reputation for its corrupting influence, especially over young people coming in from the provinces in search of 'London's streets of gold'. So Eldin and his youth leaders established an outreach within its borders. One of their music bands, called 'The Believers', was the spearhead. Much to their 'happy surprise, a serendipity one might say, the owner of one of the night-clubs invited 'The Believers' to perform in his club, and this was followed by him expressing a genuine interest in the gospel. Many of the young people in his club became Christians, some later entered training for the ministry. Sadly this friendly club owner could not come to terms with his sexual problems as a homosexual, and eventually committed suicide.

The 'honeypot' attracts wasps

Because of KT's prominent position in Notting Hill Gate, and the open-air meetings that were held on the church forecourt, the church was visited by a variety of unusual people; stories best told in Eldin's own words.

'On one occasion a man came into my vestry. He sat opposite me. As I looked at him I recognised that there was something strange about him. I noticed that he had a sixpenny piece in his hand. Then much to my surprise I saw that he had bent it in half. It became obvious that he had no ordinary problem. Suddenly he leapt to his feet. Then he became violent. He started to smash up my desk. I quickly backed away from him until I had my back to the wall. My pulse racing, inwardly I began to plead for the Lord's protection. God certainly answered my prayer because he immediately calmed down. I was then able to pray for him and he was delivered from the demon that possessed him. Afterwards I discovered that he was a convicted paedophile and that he had been in prison for abusing children. But I'm glad to say he was wonderfully delivered and gave his life to Christ.

'On another occasion I was standing in our minor hall talking to one of the deacons, Wilburt Lambe. Wilburt was the community policeman for Notting Hill Gate.

Suddenly I became aware of a man standing by my side. As I turned to ask him what he wanted, he pointed to his mouth indicating that he was dumb. I had long become dependent on the Holy Spirit's gift of discerning of spirits. As I looked at this man the Holy Spirit revealed to me that he was not dumb through natural causes. I realised that he was possessed by a dumb spirit. So I confronted the demon in him. You can imagine my surprise when he fell to the ground and became quite violent. Not against me, but against himself. So I again commanded the demon to leave him. The man's body shook violently and without any warning a black substance came out of his mouth. It was a revolting sight. Then I was gripped by severe stomach pains, and I began to vomit. I had never seen anything like it and I hope I shall never see such a thing again. The stench was nauseating. I was so sick that I had to leave the hall. Eventually I recovered and returned to the hall, and with Wilbert's help I cleared up the mess. Then to my great relief I found the man was now speaking normally. He was saying, "I want help, I want help." And there and then I led him to the Lord.

'Afterwards he told me that he'd been involved in a black magic circle in Notting Hill, and that one evening he found he was completely dumb. Since that time he hadn't been able to speak. It was, as I had perceived, demonic power. However, it ended with a wonderful victory. He was Irish and when he eventually went back to Ireland I was able to link him with one of the Irish churches.

'We also saw many people healed. On one occasion a woman came for prayer. Her face was such an awful sight that I found it difficult even to look at her. Her face had been eaten away by a cancerous growth. She had to use a scarf in an attempt to conceal it. We prayed for her but nothing seemed to happen. However, six months later she wrote to say that shortly after I prayed for her, she was completely healed.

'KT has always been a "honey pot" for freaks. But I had always believed that this was an important part of our ministry. Sometimes it was not without embarrassment because some of the public who visited our services didn't understand this, and blamed our pentecostal beliefs. There was an occasion when we had an inter-denominational choir from Bournemouth. It was a very powerful evening and there had been an anointing of the Spirit on the ministry. We were almost at the end of the service and as I began to give a gospel invitation a man ran along the back of the balcony. He rushed down the steps towards the front of the balcony and dived over the balcony rail. He flew through the air with his arms out-stretched. To my horror he hit the ground with a resound-ing thud. He was wearing a black cloak which billowed out, so afterwards we referred to him as "batman". I thought that he'd killed himself.

'Of course, there was tremendous consternation as you can imagine. As it was a special guest night the church was full. We always had doctors and nurses in the con-gregation so they rushed to his side. But as his face was getting redder and redder we recognised that his tie had tightened around his neck and try as we would we couldn't loosen it. So I ran into the church kitchen to find a knife to cut his tie loose. I found one but didn't realise the sight I presented as I rushed down the aisle brandishing this carving knife! I hadn't given it a second thought as a horrified congregation watched me insert the knife under the tie.

'Eventually we released him just as the ambulance arrived. The ambulance men could not persuade the man to accompany them. So one of my elders said to him, "You either go to the hospital, or you go to the police station—make the choice." So he went to the hospital and discovered he'd broken both his arms. It was a miracle he didn't break his neck. The leader of the choir, who was an elder in one of Elim's churches, was very troubled because he thought the people in the choir would think this was a Pentecostal manifestation that had gone wrong. So I went to the coach and apologised to the members of his choir for any embarrassment they might have had. But one of the choir called out, "Don't worry about it, Mr Corsie. We never see anything like this in Bournemouth!"'

One of the lessons to be learned in the quest for church growth is that KT had to be willing to adopt an 'open arms policy' to all who would come. Even so, there were moments of high humour.

On one occasion the pastors in the pulpit suddenly became aware of a strangely dressed man in the middle of the congregation. His name was Caverner. He was an Irish guy who used to wear an old chauffeur's hat and a duffel coat. There were empty gaps where his teeth should be. Although he was prone to act in a peculiar way the KT folk always welcomed him.

One Sunday night a couple of Hell's Angels fully dressed in their bizarre leather gear and occult badges came into the church and sat in the transept. Lyndon was preaching. One of them took a cigarette from his pocket, lit it and began to smoke. They also had two large cans of Guinness which they put under their seat.

So Eldin, who is by no means a muscular man, descended from the platform and sat beside them. Then, in as stern a voice as he could muster, reminiscent of his army days, said, 'I command you In the name of Jesus to put your cigarette out this instant.' He fully expected one of them to lift him shoulder high and throw him into the aisle. Instead they did as he said and sat there for the rest of the service without moving.

But Eldin hadn't bargained for what was to follow. When the meeting came to an end they got up and towered over him with menacing gestures as if they were going to beat him up. It so happened that also in the church that evening was one of the new converts. Before he joined KT he had been a bouncer in a Glasgow nightclub. Seeing Eldin's predicament he rushed across the church to defend him. But he was a sufferer of epilepsy and prone to attacks in unexpected moments. In his excitement he had a fit, and fell full length on the floor scattering chairs in every direction. To make matters worse his face was convulsed in a series of violent twitches. Even for those who knew him it was a frightening sight, but the effect on the Hell's Angels was sensational! The colour drained from their faces, they put up their hands in horror, leapt over the fallen chairs and ran for their lives.

Kensington Temple could not be more strategically and conveniently placed. Buses and taxis are virtually on the doorstep, and trains are just a couple of hundred metres away, serving all the mainline railway stations. The accessibility of Notting Hill Gate to the City of London and the West End makes it highly attractive for people of all walks of life. But the downside is that as a well-known meeting place it seems to have more than its fair share of drunks and people high on drugs. And it was not always easy to deal with them.

KT was also surrounded by witches' covens who were constantly making threats against the members. At the end of one Sunday evening service Eldin gave the customary invitation for anyone seeking Christ to walk to the front of the church. One young man close to the front of the church responded. On either side at the front of the church are transepts. Suddenly he began to cry out, 'Don't. Don't. Go away!' Eldin and Lyndon noticed that he was looking towards one of the transepts. Eventually Lyndon led the young man into the minor hall. After a short while Lyndon returned to tell Eldin that the young man had seen an evil spirit coming from a man in the transept. It was attacking him. Eldin looked in the direction of the transept and saw this man. He had an evil look on his face. So Eldin left the pulpit and confronted him. He just sneered at Eldin, turned and ran out of the church. Though the demon-possessed man in the transept hadn't met the man being counselled, the demon was aware that he had been involved in black magic and spiritism. And here the demon was actually transmitting his evil spirit-power in an attempt to prevent him submitting himself to Christ. But the demon failed and the young man was delivered from the occult and came through to a wonderful experience of salvation. On these occasions the Temple ministers knew that KT was in the 'front line' of the fight with the evil forces of Notting Hill.

One morning in the early seventies, when Eldin and Lyndon took their seats on the platform, they sensed that there was a strange presence in the church. As the organist was playing a devotional melody they asked the Lord to show them what was wrong. Eldin, in particular, had a very strong conviction that there was someone present who was a spiritist. Addressing the congregation Eldin said, 'I know there's a person here who is heavily involved in spiritism.' Immediately there was a commotion in one of the transepts and a woman shouted 'You mean spiritualism.' Eldin said firmly, 'No madam, there's nothing spiritual about what you practise. It's spiritism.'

The woman became very agitated and called out, 'I tell you it is spiritualism. I know. I'm a medium.' Whereupon Eldin challenged her in the name of Jesus. She got up from her seat and ran. She ran down the aisle and out of the church, slamming the doors as she went. These encounters with evil spirits attempting to disrupt the work of KT were very frequent in the sixties and seventies. The gift of the discerning of spirits was an invaluable aid to Eldin.

On another occasion, just as Eldin approached the rostrum to preach, he experienced a very disturbing sensation of evil power. He called on the congregation to pray and for any spiritists to reveal themselves. Immediately five people stood to their feet and hurriedly made their way to the front of the church where the pastors prayed for their deliverance.

Unexpected happy encounters

One of the features of KT, not only during Eldin's ministry but also the ministries of Wynne and Colin, was the training of nationals from other countries. This training was to prepare them for leadership in their home countries. This had some surprises for KT's pastors when they travelled abroad, and on many occasions they were to discover how far-reaching was KT's influence.

One time Eldin was called to visit an Elim mission station in Tanzania, and when he was there he was taken into bush country. En route they stopped at a small hospital. 'I know the people here,' said the missionary, 'so let's stop and see if they'll give us a cup of tea.'

Eldin got out of the cab and followed the missionary to the hospital entrance. Quite unexpectedly they were approached by a heavily bearded young man who, on seeing Eldin, threw up his hands and exclaimed, 'Pastor

Corsie. What on earth are you doing here?' Eldin had no idea who this young man was. 'Don't you remember me?' 'I must confess I don't,' said Eldin. The young man's beard and very long hair probably made that difficult. 'I came to your church when I was a medical student at St Thomas' Hospital in London. I was converted and filled with the Spirit at KT and then later I felt called to the mission field. I'm now working here in this hospital in Tanzania.'

Then there was the time when Eldin was walking along one of the streets in Singapore. He was a delegate at a charismatic conference. Suddenly he felt a tap on his shoulder. He turned around and there were two Chinese girls smiling at him. 'Hello, Pastor Corsie, what are you doing in Singapore?' they asked. He had to confess that he had no idea who they were. It turned out that they had been trainee nurses at St Charles' Hospital in North Kensington, and as a result of Eldin giving an address at a nurses' meeting at their hospital they began to attend KT. They were Buddhists at the time. But, after hearing about Jesus in these meetings, they invited Christ into their lives. After completing their training they returned to Singapore, and had joined an evangelical church.

'Oh God, when will you revive this church?'

From his youth Eldin had been taught by Pentecostal pastors, so he has never doubted the value of speaking in tongues. However, he was astonished by what happened at an early Sunday morning prayer meeting at the Temple. He was quietly praying in tongues, which he did frequently. However, after this particular meeting, and without warning, a man who had been in the same prayer meeting spoke to him in a foreign language. Eldin said in English, 'I don't understand what you are saying.' 'But you must be able to understand me,' said the man. 'You were speaking in my home language.' 'Where are you from?' asked Eldin. He replied, 'I'm from Greece, and you were speaking in modern Greek.' Naturally this excited Eldin and he quickly said, 'Please tell me what I've been saying.' He said, 'You kept on saying, "Oh God, when will you revive this church?".'

One morning two girls were returning to their homes in New Zealand. They had been attending KT regularly for three years. The day before they were due to leave, there was a message in tongues which was immediately interpreted. It said, 'You have collected together your goods. You have amassed your wealth. But these things will disintegrate around you in fire. Nevertheless, in that moment you will know the Lord is with you.' One of the deacons wondered if the Temple was going to be destroyed by fire.

Nothing more was said, and the next morning the girls went off to Heathrow airport. Eldin and several of his church members went to the airport with them. 'We were standing on the airport observation platform and saw the aircraft take off,' said Eldin. 'When it got to about 8,000 feet, one of the engines burst into flames. The pilot quickly brought the aircraft around and came back along the runway with fire blazing fiercely along one wing. It was a frightening sight. Five died in that fire but the New Zealand girls escaped alive. Later one of them said to me, "Do you remember what was said yesterday in the morning service? As my feet touched the tarmac after sliding down the escape shoot, I remembered the prophecy of yesterday morning." They lost everything but, as the prophecy promised, the Lord was with them and their lives were saved.'

Kensington Temple has featured in several radio and television broadcasts both BBC and ITV. On the first occasion the service included Communion. True to custom the elders with the three pastors who were taking part, stood around the Communion table. As the cameras zoomed in, one of the elders, Len Rammell, felt inspired to speak in tongues but not in a loud voice. However, it was loud enough for viewers to hear him. As Len spoke his body swayed a little, not unlike the Jewish custom during prayer. After the broadcast KT received calls from astonished viewers wondering if this 'temple' was a Jewish sect!

Eldin was used to a 'revivalist' style of worship in church. The prophetic ministry and free exercise of spiritual gifts was something with which he was fully accustomed. In fact, he was foremost among Elim ministers in promoting their use in all the churches he pastored. It was something that he fervently believed. But when you get a large congregation, as it is today, it's very difficult for all of them to hear someone giving a word of prophecy when that person may be high up in the balcony. So it became necessary to ask people to refrain from participating in this way. Ultimately, the weekly bulletin carried a notice which said, 'If you're not a member of this church please don't attempt to exercise spiritual gifts.' For those who complained that the Holy Spirit was being quenched, they would be reminded that according to the Scriptures, 'the spirit is subject to the prophet'.

To be a good leader one has to delegate. In that sense one can, in a healthy way, divide to grow. Eldin Corsie found that with the growth of the church he had to look regularly for emerging talent and make room for their gifts to be used. It was, no doubt, one of the strengths of his ministry. Lyndon Bowring would sometimes say in jest, 'Eldin thinks up the ideas. He then passes them on to me to develop. And as John Harris was the best organiser I would pass them on to him to carry them out.' That diversity also meant developing several areas of ministry, in addition to what was done from the pulpit. One of the loyal and efficient members, Dorothy Rammell, was invited to commence a bookstall at the rear of the church. Like the growth in the church, so the bookshop grew. Today it has a turnover greater than many of the UK's Christian bookshops.

The Apostles' teaching

Probably the most frequently asked question, especially by visiting pastors, is, 'What is the secret of your success?' When planning this book I was aware that this was a question that should be seriously considered. So I decided to include in this story of KT as much as possible of the thoughts of three of the principal pastors. That doesn't mean that they were the only ones to give valuable contributions to the success of the church. There have been very many other pastors, elders and members, female as well as male, without whom this story could not have been told. However, this book could not possibly have room to include them all. I have talked at length to all three pastors, Eldin Corsie, Wynne Lewis and Colin Dye, for their stories and philosophies. I can say that with the advantage of hindsight I can now see the wisdom of God's choice of these particular men, and the order in which they were chosen. Eldin was the gentle, patient and thoughtful foundation builder. Wynne was the thrusting risk-taker who made a virtue out of impatience. Colin was, and is, a mixture of both which he has cemented with long periods of prayer.

Colin's ministry at KT spanned the ministries of both Eldin and Wynne so I was interested to hear him say, 'Before Wynne took over I would describe Eldin's time at KT as the foundation years. Everything that we did and saw happen under Wynne was founded in Eldin's time. Even the satellite churches. They were then called area fellowships. There were several of them in West London. At that time we also saw the need for reaching the international community, although in those days the major ethnic grouping outside the Europeans were Chinese.'

That foundation was based on sound teaching from the Scriptures. There is no substitute for a solid foundation in Christian doctrine, otherwise, like the house built on shifting sand, it would not endure once the winds of adversity begin to blow. And winds of adversity have blown with bitter ferocity on KT. However, just as the leaders of the first Christian church in Jerusalem were quick to recognise the need for believers to be firmly grounded in doctrine, so Eldin was diligent in providing sound Bible study. The early Christians 'joined with the other believers and devoted themselves to the apostles' teaching and fellowship' (Acts 2:42, NLT).

A sound foundation is the first essential for spiritual growth, and I believe that is one of the secrets of today's phenomenal growth at Kensington Temple. As Eldin Corsie says, he placed his emphasis on expository preaching, and this he adopted as one of his fundamentals for the sound building up of the church. The exposition of Scripture means an accurate and detailed examination and explanation book by book, chapter by chapter and verse by verse. This also includes a comparative treatment of the subjects that are unearthed as the teacher proceeds through each book. Many of the Hebrew and Greek words combine several shades of meaning which the English translators from the days of Wycliffe and Tyndale could not always include in one word. This approach to Bible teaching calls for a lot of time, digging for the rich truths God's word contains, and this demands concentration and perseverance.

'As I reflect on those early years at KT,' says Eldin, 'I reckon that the reason why I placed a great deal of emphasis on expository Bible teaching was the result of studying the ministry and preaching of Dr Martyn Lloyd-Jones of Westminster Chapel. I really wanted to preach like him. He was my model. This style of ministry is what I believed the people needed. So we avoid hobby horses and the practice of preaching from favourite texts. Following his example I adopted the practice of dealing with biblical passages as and when they would arise, and I asked those who came on to the team to do the same. I believe in digging out the meaning of the text rather than just skimming over the surface.'

During one of my conversations with Dr Lloyd-Jones he expressed the opinion that the lack of Bible teaching at the time of the 1904 Welsh revival may well have been the cause for its early demise.

*Wynne
Lewis*

Wynne Lewis boasts that he and his brother and two sisters had the cleanest feet in the Welsh village of Pontyates nestled in the Gwendreth Valley between Llanelli and Carmarthen in West Wales where he was born. It was a case of self-preservation, because the four shared the same bed and that meant for all four to get into bed they had to sleep head to toe. Wynne's arrival in this small Welsh cottage coincided with the days of depression in Wales during the notorious 'thirties'. His parents were already poor; his father was forced to eke out a meagre living working underground in the coal mines. It was a hard time to raise four children. The only running water in their village was from the pump in the market square. He was not aware that houses had indoor toilets until he came to England! The family lavatory in Wales was usually called *Ty Bach*, Welsh for 'Little House', because it was placed at the bottom of the garden to be as far from the house as possible. But Wynne's home was a happy one, and he was raised in an atmosphere of prayer.

His father had to be at the coal face in the local underground mine by six o'clock every morning, but he never failed to spend an hour and a half in prayer and Bible study before leaving his little cottage. It is no wonder that

Wynne is an early riser. He's usually in his office by 7 am. But Wynne had his cross to bear. The early Pentecostalists would have nothing to do with sport. So Wynne was frequently heard to pray, 'Dear Lord, where did I get this wonderful love for rugby and cricket? Is it my thorn in the flesh?' I wonder what his forebears would say if they knew he now belongs to the London Rugby Club and is a member of the MCC (Middlesex Cricket Club).

In view of Wynne's almost fanatical interest in cricket, something short of a miracle was to happen to him during his time at KT. One of the England cricket team, Wilf Slack, began to attend the church. Wilf was not only an England Test cricketer but he was the revered opening batsman for Middlesex County Cricket Club. Sadly, when only in his early thirties he collapsed on the cricket field and died. His funeral service was held in KT and was attended by 700–800 cricketers. They included five former England captains, the whole of the England selection committee and the hierarchy of the Marylebone Cricket Club.

Wynne conducted the service and preached the sermon. Many of the cricketers were so impressed and moved that they came to Wynne after the service to tell him so. The most important result of this special event at KT was that it gave Wynne an entrée into the lives of many of the cricketers. This friendship with the team later enabled Wynne to build bridges of friendship to others.

'It was a great occasion even though a sad loss to the church and to cricket to lose this man,' reflects Wynne. 'But to see all those professional cricketers in one building, and especially in Kensington Temple, was quite something. It was probably unique in the history of cricket and certainly KT.'

It is said that a boy's hero reveals more about the boy than the hero. The hero in the life of schoolboy Wynne's life was a man called Eli Sibley. He was a coal miner-cum-pastor in Tonyryfail in the Rhondda Valley who had a style all of his own: a Welsh version of Smith Wigglesworth. His congregation used to say that if you deleted all the 'hallelujahs' and 'praise the Lords' from his sermon, his ninety-minute or so sermons would only last half an hour. But he was a great man of faith and believed God for anything. One day the cat in his house walked past Mrs Sibley as she was ironing her husband's shirts. It was a heavy flat iron. Suddenly it slipped from her hand and fell on the cat, breaking its back. Nothing daunted, Eli picked up both flat iron and cat. He got out his bottle of anointing oil and anointed the cat. He then placed his huge work-a-day hands on the whimpering animal and prayed. With an authority like the godly men of the early Church, he commanded the cat to be healed. Immediately, and to the consternation of his wife, the cat jumped out of his hands as if electrified, and scampered off into the garden perfectly whole.

However, young Wynne was not a promising preacher and very shy in those early days. When he entered the pulpit to preach his first sermon he had a large black Bible and sixteen sheets of closely written notes. He told me that he was through his sermon in four minutes flat! 'I didn't have the sense to close my Bible and return to the pews. I just stood there transfixed, immobilised, petrified, saying under my breath, "Lord, a fine mess you've got me into. I told you I was no good for this work. What do I do now?"

'The Lord said to me, "Just tell them that I've called you into the ministry." And I replied, "That's a dirty blow below the belt, that is. Why can't I tell them when I've got thirty-two sheets of notes and can last eight minutes, or better still, sixty-four sheets and talk for sixteen minutes?"'

But he plucked up the courage to tell the congregation

that he believed God had called him to the ministry. At the end of the service one of the Welsh patriarchs of the village took Wynne aside and said, 'Young man, would you take a word of advice?' Wynne readily agreed. 'If I were you, I wouldn't bother with the ministry. And I'll give you another bit of advice for nothing. You would be just about the last person God would call into the ministry. Your father is a coal miner, and your grandfather was a coal miner, and that's where you belong, my son.' Young Wynne impishly replied, 'Thank you, sir. That's what I've been telling God but he won't listen. So would you have a word with *him*?'

Wynne has since pastored some of the largest and most challenging churches in the Elim denomination and was eventually appointed its Director of Evangelism. There is no doubt that God had planned for him to come to KT. But Wynne laid down a number of formidable conditions. He had been warned that the Church Board would be slow to make a decision as to his suitability. They were also likely to say that before they could come to a decision they would need some months of prayer. If that wasn't enough to discourage him he was told that there were some elders who were opposed to his appointment. In spite of this Wynne asked God to confirm this appointment by making the Church Board's decision unanimous. And, contrary to predictions to the contrary, that is exactly what happened.

He later heard that one of the elders had said to his fellow elders, 'If you want an easy smooth ride, don't have him. On the other hand, if you want an exciting time and hope to see this place full, this is your man.'

The beginning of a fantastic pilgrimage

On the first Sunday of September 1980 Wynne Lewis entered KT's pulpit for the first time as its pastor without the customary service of induction. It was not a deliberate decision—it just happened. And that is characteristic of Wynne's ministry. He is not attracted to ceremonies and customs. As a man of action, always on the move, he was only too keen to get on with the job in hand. When he is convinced of the direction of God's will for him he plunges into action immediately and without ceremony.

Colin Dye had a ringside seat.

'Wynne came into KT and took it by the scruff of the neck! Absolutely, not even gently! Totally, immediately, decisively, conclusively by the scruff of the neck. He had the reputation of being ruthless. But he was ruthless in the things that counted—things that mattered. On the other hand he could be loving with the people, especially in the presentation of his sermons, even when he had hard things to say. Frankly none of us knew how Wynne got away with all that he did. I think that the people saw that he was a pastor at heart, and his relationship with them was lovable and genuine. His style was so different that for a while we thought the church was going in a totally different direction.'

One of the first tasks Wynne set himself was to reshape the Church Board. He felt the eldership was too busy with petty details. He believed that they should not be involved with the minutiæ of finances; the colour of carpets and walls. These were the duties of deacons, and he had scriptural authority for this. 'Let the deacons get on with such things,' he would say, 'the elders should concentrate on the spiritual progress of the church; on vision and growth. That's where I need their help.'

Wynne set out his principles, a philosophy for growth, in one of his first sermons. 'I remember it well,' says Colin. 'I was there. He preached on the church at Antioch. He drew illustrations from that early church to describe what sort of church he felt KT should be. It should be a sending church—and that is how KT has developed. We can now look back with the benefit of hindsight and see that everything he said in that sermon, which was his manifesto, was taken up and fulfilled. He definitely knew where he was going.'

Browsing through the early church magazines I discovered that Elder Len Rammell had been diligent in his work as editor and summarised Wynne's sermon under the title 'The Ideal Church'. Len, in his introduction, posed the question: 'What kind of church would he [Wynne] like Kensington Temple to be? He saw the New Testament Antioch church as the prototype church. What were the characteristics of Paul's home church?' This is Len's summary of Wynne's answers.

'It was a spiritual church. Pentecostal, and open to the moving of the Holy Spirit without countenancing fanaticism. Prepared for routine to be interrupted, and always open to the word of God.

'It was a worshipping church, with Jesus Christ being the focal point.

'It was a fasting and praying church. We debated, said Wynne, but they fasted and prayed. This was a much safer way. Crucial decisions need to be taken by spiritual methods.

'It was a church with outreach. Satan would be happy if he could confine us to the limits of the KT building. Satan always sought to confine and contain the fire of God. We need the wind of God with which to spread the flame of the gospel. Antioch saturated the area with the gospel and we need to develop means of penetrating the indifference of the areas of Notting Hill and Kensington.

'It was a church with a world vision. I will not be happy until KT has a ring of daughter churches.

'It was a church with a training programme in discipleship. We are called to make disciples and to train teachers.

'It was a church aware of the need for multiple ministries. The evangelists taught and the teachers evangelised. Kensington Temple never has been, nor will be, a "one man band".

'It was a church with a commitment to people. They loved the Lord and each other too!

'It was a church that allowed nothing to stop its progress. Winning souls was more important than winning a debate. Personal progress was more important than personal views.'

As I read those targets I recognised how they had and are being achieved.

Colin was profoundly moved by that sermon and deeply touched by Wynne's great warmth for the people. He saw him in a new light, a lovable person. Eldin was a caring, lovable pastor, but Wynne showed his concern in a different way. Of course, he didn't suffer fools gladly, so it's not surprising that he had a reputation for being rude and unsympathetic. However, he would frequently get away with this direct style of preaching by his humour. On one occasion the BBC came to make a documentary on KT for their Sunday evening programme *Everyman*. The crew said they had never seen a church or a pastor like this. 'Pure theatre,' they commented.

Can impatience be a virtue?

Wynne readily admits that he is an impatient man. Colin agrees: 'Wynne is not patient. In fact he makes a virtue out of his impatience!' Wynne confesses, 'I want everything done overnight. Everything's got to happen straight away.' As if to emphasise the point Wynne admits, 'I'm not a great democrat. I have a strong belief that the church and democracy don't mix. But that doesn't mean I like dictatorship or autocracy. When people say that theocracy is the right government in the church, I say that's fine but God doesn't always have his own way—we don't allow him. So I would say it's benevolent dictatorship that I believe in. I have a feeling that if I don't hear from God what needs to be done, I have no right to be the leader. The leader must always be several steps ahead of his followers. But I don't bypass elders and deacons, because if I can't convince twelve or eighteen people after I have told them, "This is what I've heard from God," how can I convince the rest of the church?

'When I address conferences of ministers I am often asked if I had a vision of what KT was going to be like. Well, I'm not very much into visions. I don't disagree with them, but I don't find them happening to me that often. I use the phrase, "faith statements". Don't misunderstand me; it's not snatching figures from the air. But in one's walk with God I believe it's right to ask, "Lord, where should the church be in twelve months time?" Then when you hear from God you make a statement that encourages the people. When you talk about growth and the people can see growth happening, even though it may be gradual, they can believe that the upward curve can go even steeper. That helps you to inject faith.' Wynne leaned forward in his chair. 'Jack, you say in your book on the life of Smith Wigglesworth, that the first thing Wigglesworth would do in his meetings would be to raise the faith of the people, *then* he would preach and pray for the sick. And that is exactly what I believe.'

Wynne planned that KT should increase by twenty-five per cent in that first year. The people were willing to give him his head. He found them a caring people; that was one of the hallmarks of Eldin, his predecessor. He was, and still is, such a caring man, and the congregation reflected that. Wynne says, 'I've never met a congregation more loving, kind and caring than KT.'

There were 300–400 people in the congregation for his first Sunday morning, and they included between thirty and forty different nationalities. The aggregate for the day, Eldin tells me, would have been around 600. Almost immediately, as Wynne sat looking out into the body of the church (the balcony was not used in those days), he heard God say, 'Look around you and what do you see?' 'The whole world,' replied Wynne. 'Yes,' that inner voice continued. 'And I want KT to reach out to the whole world. I want this to be a place where young men and women from all the countries of the world are trained and then return to their homelands as my ambassadors.'

So, in obedience to that word from God, Wynne decided to give priority to two particular goals. He decided that he would begin a programme to make KT an international church and also a 'sending' church. And with all those nationalities present those targets seemed to fit.

Lyndon comments, 'Half the Ghanian cabinet of the ousted government in the seventies ended up in London. They were almost all barristers and lawyers. Five of them came to worship at KT, including the Ministers of Interior and Defence. Many returned to Ghana like Kwako Boateng, father of Paul Boateng, the present Minister of Social Services. Kwako stood in the presidential elections of Ghana and came a close second to the man who is now its president. There were also princes and princesses of leading African countries in the congregation. We frequently had Arab dignitaries passing through London from their home countries where public proclamation of the gospel was forbidden, so their identity had to be hidden. They would come to KT to have their spiritual "batteries" recharged before returning to their homeland.'

Wynne began to enlist an army of men and women to help fulfil the task. Every week new faces appeared. Visiting preachers came to widen the vision of the congregation.

On one occasion Wynne was visiting the largest Pentecostal church in Malaysia when he received encouraging evidence of the fulfilment of God's instruction that KT should be a sending church. 'One of the great joys today, when I'm travelling around the world, is to see pastors of some of the largest churches in the world who first found Christ in KT.' When these remarkable events began to happen it was evident that KT was no ordinary church; it was quite unlike any church that Wynne Lewis had previously pastored. What were his feelings at the time?

During the early years of his ministry at KT there was steady growth but not enough to satisfy him. Then suddenly his life, and the life of the church, was turned upside down. There was a dramatic intervention in his life which led to a remarkable conversation with God.

'I was coming home one night on the M1, when a lady in a very fast sports car had a tyre blow out and she hit my car. As my car rolled over the embankment and down the sharp, steep incline I thought I would soon be singing Jim Reeve's song "Lord I'm coming home". But it wasn't to be, thank God. It seemed as if I'd got away very lightly from that bad smash. However, it left me with a residual weakness in my back.

'To cut a long story short, in 1983 I went in for a spinal operation with the result that I was in and out of hospital for six months. Then infection got into the spine. I thought, "Lord, I'm never going to be able to walk again, I'm paralysed." So I sent for my senior elder, Len Rammell. I said, "Len, I'm finished. Call the elders and get them to appoint a new minister." He was obviously shocked.

'Just twenty-four hours later he was back. "We've had

an elders' meeting," he said, "and we want you to know that if you never preach again, you're our senior minister for life." Now that was an amazing thing for someone to say. And that bucked me up no end.

'I had been very depressed. I was paralysed. I remember one morning in hospital, it was about quarter to three, I was in agony. I rang the bell and an Australian nurse came and I pleaded with her, "Please pump some more pain killers into me, I'm in agony." When she looked at my chart she said, "Reverend, you can't have any more." So I prayed, "Lord, if this is it, you can just take me. Take me home now." But just then the thought came to me. "Are you trying to say something to me, Lord? Are you trying to speak to me?" Then I distinctly heard God say to me, "Yes, Wynne." "Then tell me what are you trying to say?" I said. You can imagine my astonishment, knowing KT from those early days, when God said to me, "I've been looking for someone who will build me a church of 5,000 in London." I could hardly believe what I was hearing, but I responded, "OK Lord, if you'll spare me, and if you'll heal me, then here I am. You do with me as you will." But then he showed me the price tags—which were pretty steep.

'One of them was that he wanted me to write a letter. "You've got a dictating machine in your locker. Dictate a letter to all the members and friends of the Temple. Have it distributed morning and evening for four Sundays in a row. Apologise for being a bad pastor."'

'I said, "Lord, I haven't been a bad pastor. I love the people. Look at the growth. Church growth people have been writing about it." But God said, "What do they know about growth? Most of them are analysts and haven't done it. Twenty per cent growth! If you had learnt to do my work in my way, in my time, I could have given you one hundred per cent growth overnight. If you will respond to my challenge and do things my way, I will accomplish far greater things at Kensington Temple than you have imagined."

'And there I began on a fantastic pilgrimage with the Holy Spirit where he became more real than ever.

'Initially I thought that when God said 5,000 he was referring to *a building seating* 5,000. So we made an offer for the old White City Stadium in West London that had just come onto the market. But, of course, that was sold for £32 million—far beyond our league! But the Lord said, "No. I didn't say a building. I said a central church with 5,000." So I said, "Lord, how?"

'When I was discharged from hospital, I asked one of our elders who came to drive me home, "Take me down to the church first. I haven't been there for six months."

'It was a Wednesday afternoon, about 3.30 pm, and getting darkish. I stood on the lower platform and it was then that the Lord gave me a vision. It's probably the only major vision I've had in my whole life. The Lord showed me the building with every seat full and thousands being turned away. In the darkness of that winter afternoon I heard a voice say, "Is that de pastor?" It was Florence, our African princess who held two portfolios in the Ugandan government before the days of Idi Amin. She was somewhere in the shadows of that unlit church. She shouted, "Where have you been, Pastor Wynne?" She hadn't been told that I was in hospital and because I was absent from the pulpit she thought I was away preaching. She then went on to say that for the past two months the Lord had been showing her a picture of the church full to capacity. In her customary blunt manner she added, "What are you going to do about it?"

'That was sufficient confirmation for me.

'Having had that vision, which was vertical, I then had

to strategise. I said, "Lord, how is this to happen?" He replied, "Get up to Marble Arch." I went up at nine o'clock one morning, and God said, "What do you see?" I said, "People of all colours, all races." It then began to dawn on me that many of the home countries of these people were closed to the gospel, but God had brought them to London as students or as diplomats. God told me, "Now win them, train them, send some of them back."'

It is necessary to mention here that though the balcony of the church had been used on many occasions during Eldin's ministry, during Cliff Richard's visit for example, it had fallen into disuse. The result was that it had become a repository for broken chairs, among other things. But as a result of the vision God had given him, Wynne felt that he should take steps to make the balcony usable again.

'I remember saying to the elders,' he reminisced, '"Now we've got to clear all that junk out." And they said, "What for?" I said, "For the growth that God has shown me that is to come." They didn't seem ready to agree with me at first. "Well," they said, "let's fill downstairs first." But I had a strong conviction that we should begin to empty the balcony immediately.'

So Wynne said, 'No, let's empty the balcony of that junk now!' Wynne was determined to have his own way. 'I've got a reputation for having my own way,' said Wynne. He is aware that this has given him a bad reputation with some people. However, he also knows that when he's convinced that God wants him to do a certain thing, it becomes a priority in his life and he'll suffer no opposition, even though it may appear unspiritual to others.

'You see, that's where a lot of people go wrong,' Wynne adds. 'Long before growth occurs one has to put in the infrastructure. Now the remarkable thing that followed that conversation was that as we cleared each section of the balcony and installed new seats, within three to four months that section was full. Ultimately the ushers had to put up a notice to say, "No more seats. The house is full." That was an exciting time. But that was not all. The Lord added, "That's only the beginning."'

Soon Wynne found himself in the middle of another dilemma. His problem was not to fill empty chairs. Instead, his difficulty was to find enough seats for the hundreds that the ushers were forced to turn away. So again he launched another ambitious programme, even though he encountered opposition from some of the elders. He decided that the only way to provide extra room was to excavate below the church floor and into church foundations. At the same time the floor of the church would need to be raised. That called for an enormous amount of finance—half a million pounds.

Sunday's numbers treble

During the first six years of Wynne's pastorate at KT he had witnessed an astonishing move of God. The Sunday congregations had more than trebled. There were almost 2,000 people coming into KT on Sunday mornings alone. To help in the expansion he enrolled several assistant pastors, supported by twelve elders and twenty-five deacons, and by this time there were upwards of 100 different nationalities in the congregation.

In what must have been the understatement of the year, Wynne told one reporter, 'I suppose I've always been slightly radical in my views. But the lesson God was teaching me was that a large church must be even more open to change than a small one. You see a large fellowship will cruise on its own momentum for a while. If you cut a branch off a tree it will send out extra shoots because of the residual sap, but if it does not receive an adequate supply of moisture it will dry out eventually.'

More than ever Wynne was now beginning to learn how to listen more accurately to the voice of God. This may not be as much a problem for others as for Wynne. He just cannot keep still for long. And he is never happier than when surrounded by a host of milling people. One of the many alterations he made to the inside of the building was to provide a large office for himself, perhaps ten metres long by five wide. Between the two morning services each Sunday he would sit, but never remain still, at his large desk with a 'Japanese-size smile' enveloping his round face. There are two doors to this office, and it seemed sometimes that the whole congregation was pouring in from both ends.

'I love people. I came into church late one morning, and as I passed my office I heard one of my secretaries say, "Mr Lewis is too busy to see you." I didn't say anything then, but I called them in afterwards and told them not to say that again. Never say that I'm too busy for people. In fact, the following Sunday I announced from the pulpit that anyone can come and see me. Maybe I'll only give them a couple of minutes, and if they can tell me what's on their heart or troubling them in that time, that's fine. But I will also pass them on to someone who has more time and can help them. Following my announcement there were queues of people at both doors after every meeting. Frequently I would not get home from the after- noon meeting until supper time! It did, however, show them that even though I had taken a step in a different direction in leadership, which appeared to override some loyal members, I was still available to them.'

After a few months when they knew that was so, he used to say to them, 'If you can't get to me at church, you can lift the phone to talk to me at any hour, night or day, if you're really in trouble.' When people knew that, they felt good because he had set out to prove that he was not merely a figure, remote, up there on the platform.

The old adage 'variety is the spice of life' was a principle Wynne Lewis was not afraid to apply to his churches. On one occasion he invited Delia Smith, the famous TV cook who has probably published more cookery books worldwide than anyone else. What is not so well known is the fact that she is also a keen Christian, and she agreed to Wynne's invitation to visit KT. Inevitably it was a great experience for the church and the place was full. Wynne is always an excellent host so he asked Lyndon Bowring to find a suitable restaurant to take Delia for a meal after the evening service. Lyndon, always economical, took the party to a humble café in a back street where they served chips and processed peas. He was unaware, until after the event, that this Delia Smith was the famous Delia Smith!

Philosophy for church growth

Wynne Lewis's philosophy for church growth is not some obscure theory. 'We are a growing church. Analysts of church growth were writing about us when I heard God say, "Wynne, you're not growing at my speed, nor in the way I want you to grow."

'The basic reason for our growth is that as a church, and especially as a leadership, we have decided to listen to the voice of God. When you really begin to do that, and are prepared to let the Holy Spirit have his way, any church can be revolutionised. We've made changes, taken risks and launched out in faith—but only when we've been convinced that it will be under God's direction. It's no good getting on to someone else's bandwagon or

Principal George Jeffreys, renowned Welsh 'revivalist', who founded the Elim Pentecostal Churches in Monaghan, Ireland in 1915. He conducted some of the largest evangelistic meetings in the UK in the first part of the 20th century.

This drawing of Horbury Chapel, later renamed Kensington Temple, appeared in the 15th September 1849 edition of *The Illustrated London News*, the week that it was opened. It was originally built without a gallery at a cost of £4,000.

1966: H.W. Greenway, General Superintendent of Elim, preaches at the first televised service from Kensington Temple. To his left sits a younger Jack Hywel-Davies. "The Elim movement was first named Elim Foursquare Churches, here summarised in the stained glass windows behind the pulpit, as 'Our Lord Jesus Christ, Saviour, Healer, Baptiser, Coming King'."

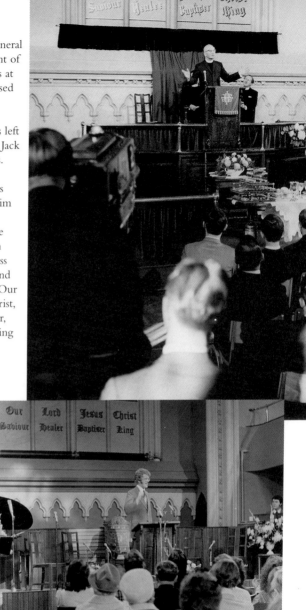

Lyndon Bowring, Chairman of CARE, as associate pastor of Kensington Temple in the 1970s. He is currently a non-executive member of the church board.

Kensington Temple undergoes a complete refit to accommodate the additional increase in the congregation during the early 1980s.

KT given more room for the increasing congregations.

Left to right: Wynne Lewis, the late Len Rammel (senior elder) and Eldin Corsie conduct the re-opening celebrations in 1982.

Eldin Corsie led his small congregation into Kensington Temple in 1965, and continued as Senior Pastor until 1980, by which time it had increased almost ten-fold.

Wynne Lewis under whose ministry from 1980 to 1991 KT saw its greatest expansion.

Colin Dye, formerly church officer, associate minister and in 1991 appointed Senior Pastor. Colin has seen the growth of the 1980s continue into the 1990s.

Richard Lewis, Director of Music at KT and former concert pianist.

Ruth-Ann Cannings, Director of Social Ministries and former nursing companion to Jacqueline du Pré.

Japanese-born Keiko Holmes has pioneered and now oversees a reconciliation programme for Britain's Japanese prisoners of war, which is now part of KT.

Carrie and David Grant, renowned vocalists of tv, radio and public concerts who founded KT's School of Creative Ministries, and continue to perform and advise at KT's music programmes.

KT's church services are
never dull. Worship and
prayer are essential elements
and lie at the heart of
Kensington Temple.

making changes just for the sake of it. That will lead to confusion. We need to listen to God—for a change!

'Well, I always say to pastors in my seminars on church growth that you've got to evaluate your area. "Are you in a working-class area? Are you in a university town or city?"' It was, and still is, Wynne's practice to tell leaders that they have to know the people they are ministering to. And church leaders must then work accordingly. He is frequently heard to say, 'It's no good going into a little village and saying, "I've got a ministry to university students" if they're not there!'

One thing Wynne did concentrate on for the first two years of his ministry at KT was to write to every Christian Union in the London colleges saying, 'I'm prepared to come and speak at your CU at any time.' For the following two years he was invited to speak at several of these colleges. We focussed our attention on students because we recognised that they were potential leaders in the future generation. Wynne defends, this saying, 'It wasn't a snobbish thing at all. In fact, I also started a cricket team. I love cricket, and we attracted many young people in this way.'

Interestingly, although Wynne was unaware of it, this was the plan that Eldin carried out fifteen years earlier. The lesson to be learned here is that if you have a good idea, it's sometimes worth repeating it though the circumstances may not be the same.

Any church can be renewed

'It really is nonsense to say that churches cannot be renewed,' says Wynne. 'A church is made up of individuals. If you can get enough of them to change you will have a renewed church. However, I believe that first of all a church must want to change. That means that the senior pastor, and that's me in the case of Kensington, has to spend a lot of time with his team of leaders. I would advise any pastor who wants to see his church grow to make this his top priority.'

One of Wynne's priorities in this area was to meet with his young pastors on a weekly basis for the first twelve months of their life at KT. In that way he was able to share the concepts that God had fed into his soul. He would constantly affirm that any church can grow if it is willing to pay the price. And it can be a heavy price. But when you are the leader you must not try and be a 'Jack of all trades'; you have to concentrate on the gifts God has given you. Reflecting on the past years Wynne told me in one of our meetings, 'I don't consider myself to be a pastor in the biblical sense of the word "shepherd"—someone who is patient and long suffering. I'm not a pastor. I'm a visionary. I'm a conceptualist. I can motivate people. I can inspire people. And I soon discovered that I had to bring people into leadership that complemented my ministry.'

I will always be grateful to the forgotten tutor at one of the colleges I attended who introduced me to the superb essays of Dr Boreham. In one he says, 'We all need makeweights.' That is, someone to compensate for our short-comings. He went on to say that wild horses would never get out of him the name of his makeweight. But that was tongue in cheek, because in the next sentence he discloses his secret. His makeweight was his wife. And one of Wynne's makeweights from the early days of his ministry in South Wales was his wife, Carol.

Wynne knew what he could do. He could plant churches. He could inspire. 'I'm not a teacher, I'm not a pastor, I'm not an administrator,' he would say. So he looked for his first 'makeweight', a Bible teacher. He was a man called Michael Carr who had been a university lecturer; a first-class teacher. Then he created a pastoral care division and put Ruth-Ann Cannings in charge. (Ruth-Ann's fascinating story appears in a later chapter of this book.) So he began a system where pastoring the pastors became an important part of his ministry. He would do this through his Wednesday morning meetings.

'That's what I mean by getting close to one's team of leaders,' says Wynne. 'We would meet from 7 am to 8 am for prayer. From 8 to 9 we would breakfast together. I'm a great believer in having fellowship around the meal table. Jesus did that. Then from 9 to 11 I would teach this team of pastors, teachers, administrators and evangelists the principles of successful leadership. This would be followed by another hour, 11 to 12, for interaction. Then we would disperse. So my pastoral role was to look after the leaders. After that I would meet with the satellite pastors and house-group leaders, and so on. That's how the church was governed and pastored. I suppose really the pastors are the home-cell leaders. They know who's hurting, who's sick, who's in hospital—that's where the pastoring is done. Sunday is only a celebration, it can only be a celebration in a large church.

'But, as I tell the leaders I now meet in my world travels, you must discover from God the key to your local situation. You can't adapt any church growth principle to any place. For example, one of the keys to our success at KT has been the fostering of international fellowships within the church. Contrary to the opinion of many we have encouraged each ethnic group to have its separate meetings and meals to which their non-Christian friends can be invited.'

'Wholesale healings' in the Temple

There was an occasion in the ministry of Smith Wigglesworth when he said that God taught him the lesson of 'wholesale healings'. When he was conducting evangelistic meetings in the parks in Sweden the police put a ban on him laying hands on people when he prayed for their healing. So he prayed for them en masse from the platform and called it 'wholesale healing ministry'. It proved to be a blessing in disguise, because as the crowds coming forward for prayer increased to such a large extent it became impossible for him to pray for everyone individually. In a similar way Wynne Lewis was to experience healings without the customary 'laying on of hands'.

'I remember one Sunday morning, I had been very desperate for a few weeks, crying to God that we needed something in the services that was more than the ordinary. I had been praying all week, "Lord, do something new in church next Sunday morning."

'The Sunday came and the morning meeting didn't seem to have anything extraordinary about it. I was about to pronounce the benediction when I heard the Lord say to me, "Look, it's nearly one o'clock and you haven't allowed me to do anything new." And I said, "Well Lord, it's nearly time to close." But he said, "Well I don't take long." Then he went on, "Tell the people that I'm about to move in a wave of miracles. Just like you see a field of ripened corn, when the wind blows the heads gently move, then you can trace the path of the wind—I'm about to move like that."

'That put me on the spot. I wondered if it was God speaking or just my wishful thinking. I said to myself, "Don't bother the people. Just announce the benediction because if nothing happens you'll have egg on your face." I don't mind telling you I really sweated. So, to give me more time to think, I asked the people to sing the closing song again. Then I took the plunge and I launched out and told the people what the Holy Spirit was impressing on me. For thirty seconds nothing happened. And thirty seconds is a long time when you're in front of a packed church. Then all of a sudden just below me in the right-hand transept of the church, a lady who had come in paralysed leapt to her feet and cried out, "I'm healed." Just like the gentle wind that the Spirit had previously described to me, people were jumping up and saying, "I'm healed of this," and, "I'm healed of that."

'Downstairs first, then it went up into the balcony. People all over the place were shouting out, "I'm healed." The last one to be healed was a six-foot-six American weight-lifter who had injured his back weight lifting. I can remember him now so vividly shouting out, "My back is healed. My back is healed. Praise God my back is healed." All this happened in the following thirty seconds. There were something like twenty-seven people who testified to healing that morning. And nobody had laid hands on them.

'I have to say that was the first time the Holy Spirit did it that way. But I remember another healing service at KT. It was Sunday evening this time. Again I felt the Lord saying, "I want you to make a faith statement. I want you to say that I will heal everybody tonight who is suffering from arthritis." Now I've never done that before or since. That night twenty people who had been suffering from arthritis stood to their feet for prayer. The Lord then said, "Don't call them out, just pray one prayer." I was not used to this, but I obeyed the voice inside me. They were all healed. Then every one of them came forward and testified that they had been healed. The way they moved their limbs left no room to doubt them.

'Now those incidents are just like the story in the Gospel of John. At the Pool of Bethesda when the angel stirred the water, the first one who entered the water was healed. It was one of those visitations. I don't think you can ever repeat those incidents unless God tells you. Because it's not an act of man—it's not horizontal, it's vertical. Normally, of course, we would carry out the injunction of James when he wrote, "If there is anyone sick among you let him call for the elders of the church. Let them anoint him with oil and pray the prayer of faith, and he will be healed." That's what we normally would have done. We ask people to come forward for prayer. But God has his own way of doing things and I'm very happy to go along with it.'

KT believes that its object is often achieved when as many of its adherents leave as enter its doors each week. It is a church of travellers. A happy bunch of Christian nomads. A high percentage are in London for a short time and it is hoped that the teaching they receive at KT will be passed on to others they meet in their travels. Because of this constant state of change any information given from the platform has to be repeated for several Sundays if there is any hope of reaching all the people. The congregations are also made up of people with varying degrees of understanding of Christian doctrine. Wynne Lewis says that it is not unusual for him to receive between ten and twenty requests for marriage services after he has given a strong biblical condemnation of extra-marital sex. This would also include couples who may be living together on a permanent basis outside marriage.

Another aspect of KT's ministry is the clear-cut manner of its presentation of the Christian's financial responsibilities, that is, the financial obligations that are placed on Christians. The evidence that people take notice is seen when the offertory is about to be received. Members do not merely empty their pockets of unwanted coins, but instead they open up their cheque books. That generosity often extends to the unexpected visitor. Recently a pastor arrived from Romania, without prior notice. When it was discovered that he was in London to buy a vehicle for his church, KT's warm-hearted people were invited to show their love by placing gifts in his pockets as they left. The pastor was instructed to stand at the door at the end of the service and you can imagine his consternation when the people kept pressing their gifts into his pockets. That morning he took £2000 back to Romania. Part of KT's success is its generosity. As the Prayer Book Collect says, 'Give full rein to every generous impulse.'

Two of KT's members returned to London from a visit to their homeland, Sri Lanka. They told a pitiful story of young children made orphans by the civil war. Today there is a brand-new children's home outside Colombo staffed by this couple and financed by KT. Wynne Lewis believes that if any one in the congregation has a call from God and can convince the Church Board and the Pastoral Team that it is genuine, KT will swing in behind him or her and provide the finance to get it on its way.

Wynne says, 'Now in hindsight I can see that this church was something special. God had a plan for it to have an impact not only on London, or the UK, but further afield. I had a sense of excitement as I felt within me that this church was significant to the kingdom of God. The Lord said to me quite plainly, "Look at all those people. I want you to build a multi-racial church because I want to influence the whole world from this church." I'm sure I'm not going too far by saying that even in this country the influence of KT in the Houses of Parliament has not yet reached its zenith. But I was also humbled. When you think of my background. Coming from a little village of about 700 people, I had been a shy, introverted youngster when I went to the Elim College in London. It really amazes me when I read of the people used by God, like Moses who protested that he wasn't good enough to confront Pharaoh, and Gideon who said to God, "Who am I to save Israel? My family has no influence in the country." I felt like that. "Why me, Lord?" But God said, "Never mind that, I've chosen you. Isn't that good enough?" I find that many leaders and other Christians waste such a lot of time analysing why God wants to use them instead of letting him use them.'

London's most multi-racial church?

For a short while I was the Director General of the Martin Luther King (UK) Foundation. My brief was to devise a programme for the enhancement of racial harmony in the wake of the assassination of Dr Martin Luther King, the Baptist pastor and Civil Rights Campaigner of Atlanta, Georgia. Integration was the campaign word of the anti-racists.

So I can imagine the consternation of the Church Board of Kensington Temple when Wynne Lewis announced that he was going to encourage the development of ethnic groups to organise their own meetings under the umbrella of KT. He believed that God told him to do this. Wynne is not racist. On the contrary he is violently opposed to racial discrimination in any form and his track record at KT proves it.

'I felt the Lord was saying, "You are to build a multi-racial church. One church where you will be a demonstration to the world, with all its cultural differences, with all its prejudices, that the gospel enables us to accept each other's foibles and understand each other." God was saying to me that day that we were to be an example to the United Nations. "Look," he said. "The gospel enables all people of all creeds, all colours and of any culture to worship me as one when they come to me through Christ." So that was all important to me. Who can gainsay the word of the Lord?'

But en route Wynne was to encounter many obstacles.

'Many of the older Filipinos didn't speak English. So we had to start a Filipino church where the language would be Tagalog. Then when the Ethiopians came and the Eritreans, many of them could not speak English so we had to start a church for them. The same applied to many of the Chinese, one of whom, Joshua Chan from Hong Kong who had been converted in London, began his church on the borders of London's Chinatown. Of course, most of the Africans could speak English.

'We wanted one church to tell people that we can get rid of this evil of racism if we work at our problems. Obviously, there are cultural differences. For instance, Pentecostalists are renowned for their prejudices. When I went first to Poland it was their Christmas time, which is January. I went to a little village on the Russian border. The first service was at four o'clock in the morning, and twenty-six degrees below. The snow was up to my hip. I thought, "Who in their right mind would come to church at 4 am on Christmas morning?" But the church was packed full!

'As I entered I noticed everybody staring at me. I asked my interpreter, "What's the matter with them? Haven't they seen a Westerner before?" "That's not the reason why they are staring at you," he said. "Didn't you notice you were the only one wearing a tie?" Astonished, I replied, "So what?" "Well," he said, "if a brother wears a tie in this church it's a sign that he's a backslider!"'

In his many world travels Wynne has visited churches where women were not allowed to wear wedding rings. In others, mixed bathing is forbidden. Many Christians have made culture a doctrine. They have sadly mistaken culture for doctrine. 'That is wrong,' said Wynne. So he believed that God wanted him to show the people at KT that there can be a variety of expressions in culture. 'There are things in my culture which might offend yours, and things in yours which offend me, but in Christ we accept each other.

'So I took these words of the Lord as marching orders, and asked him, "How do I build you a multi-racial church?" "Well," he said, "did you see those Chinese people in church on Sunday morning?" I said, "Yes." He said, "What do Chinese people like?" I thought for a moment then replied, "Fried rice, chow mein!" It had never entered my head that one could win people through what I have subsequently called "culinary evangelism", because, as far as I could see, nobody was writing about "grow your church through 'culinary evangelism'!" But this was a one off, so I thought.

'I then went to our Chinese members and asked them to cook a Chinese meal on the first Sunday of each month to which they could invite their friends: meeting first, eating afterwards. Over the next two years hundreds of Chinese people along with folk from Indonesia and Malaya began coming to KT. It was a huge success and we were greatly encouraged.'

Perhaps this is a good place to tell my story of KT's Chinese church that was the outcome of Wynne's action.

The challenge of the dragon

One of the delightful duties I carried as Superintendent of the satellite churches was to visit the fascinating ethnic groups associated with KT. The Cantonese Christians were no exception. However, it did seem odd to be preaching in English in the middle of London and to be dependent on an interpreter to make myself understood by the audience in front of me. This is what happened.

Joshua Chan is the leader of KT's Chinese fellowships. I visited his church at the northern end of London's

Chinatown, which was followed by a mouth-watering meal in one of Soho's excellent restaurants.

For the thousands of tourists who stroll through the colourful streets of Chinatown, the evil power of the Chinese dragon goes unnoticed. The pagan idols for sale hold most of the Chinese in a frightening grip, yet appear to be mere curios for the uninformed. But now Joshua and his fellow Christians have taken up the gauntlet to challenge the dragon.

Chinatown is a place for the Chinese to gather, but it has become Satan's stronghold. Joshua says that the evil atmosphere is so oppressive that it is almost tangible. Into that territory he has led his team and they have now a firmly grounded foothold on its northern border close to St Giles Circus. Their satellite church is called The Salvation for Chinese Christian Fellowship and was established in 1988. The inspiration had come from Joshua Chan's visit to the Eurofire Conference in Birmingham. He began with fifteen Chinese Christians, mainly members of his own family, and now more than one hundred attend their services.

Joshua's 'army' attacks evil in Chinatown

One day Joshua was struck by the fact that his namesake, Joshua, Israel's patriarch, led his people on a walk around the walls of Jericho, so he took his people on a 'prayer walk' around Chinatown. They followed this with setting up their own 'prayer targets' by focusing their prayers on some of the idol shops, even conducting their prayer meetings outside the shops. Within a few weeks some of the shops were forced to close through lack of business.

This not only provoked anger from the shopkeepers, but they also encountered the forces of evil. Joshua and his team were not daunted. They confronted the purveyors of evil with their own 'army', as they engaged in street evangelism. However, the team members experienced nausea and bouts of vomiting. On one of their forages into the heartland of Chinatown they found themselves in conversation with a group of surly Chinese men. They told them about the liberating power of Jesus and the Holy Spirit. As they spoke they noticed several Chinese women standing on the outskirts of the crowd, obviously interested in what was being said but too timid to venture into the group.

A week later Joshua was at home watching a TV programme about Chinatown and the underground activities of the infamous Triads. Imagine his astonishment when he recognised the Triads as men he and his fellow Christians had been witnessing to earlier in the week. The women were the prostitutes in their employ. The Triads are notorious Chinese gangsters engaged in drug-running, prostitution and 'protection' rackets.

Many other false religions and dangerous cults were confronted by Joshua and his fellow Chinese Christians. They began to see the Acts of the Apostles repeated in London's Chinatown. In one of their street meetings after Joshua described the healings that had taken place under the ministry of the Apostles, sick people came to them for prayer for healing. They were about to leave when suddenly they found themselves surrounded by people claiming to be faith-healers. 'Where did you get that power we saw around you?' asked these devil-worshippers. 'We saw clouds of power around you as you were praying over those people. We want it.'

Chinese culture

'Basically, the Chinese communities are very close,' Joshua explained. 'They are bound by ancestral worship, idol worship and superstition, and one influences the other. Their way of life and thinking is governed by what "Confucius says". Worshipping various idols is compulsory and one of the biggest stumbling blocks to young Chinese Christians. When they return to their families after becoming Christians they find themselves under the severest form of pressure from their parents to continue worshipping their ancestors. They are accused of betrayal when they refuse to do this.'

Joshua Chan arrived in England from Hong Kong in 1971. With him were not only his parents, his three brothers and three sisters, but the inevitable family idol. It was the Chinese goddess of mercy, Koon Yun'.

'Koon Yun' loses out

Joshua worked hard at school, and succeeded in gaining a place to read biochemistry at London University's Queen Mary College. God's timing is never at fault. One of his fellow students was a Christian, and he invited Joshua to a Christian meeting. To his surprise he heard himself saying, 'Yes, I'll come.' Then, for him, the unexpected happened. During the meeting he sensed a strange and awesome presence around him. Today he knows that 'presence' was the Spirit of God. It was a 'Damascus road' experience. Returning to his rooms he could not escape the sensation. Not that he was inclined to. It was warm and reassuring, yet unsettling. The next day he asked his college friend to tell him more about Jesus and his way of life.

So began the story of a Chinese family turning from their pagan gods to Christ. Within a short while Joshua had overcome the fears of his brothers and sisters about his new-found faith. Like him they were to embrace the Christian life.

His elderly parents were not so easily convinced but eventually their attitude to Jesus changed. They began to think of him as a 'kind god', even better than their Chinese gods, but they still kept their altar and could only think of Jesus as one of many gods.

The Holy Spirit comes in!

One night, after the parents had gone to bed, Joshua and his brothers and sisters held a prayer meeting in the living room. They were praying for the salvation of their parents. They also prayed for the youngest sister who, as yet, had not been baptised in the Spirit. As they laid hands on her she began to tremble. 'Then,' Joshua told us, 'her appearance changed. She no longer looked like her normal self. It was uncanny,' he added. Suddenly it dawned on them that they were not dealing with their sister, but with the evil spirit that was possessing her.

They were new to this experience. The next day their pastor came to the house and after a week of fasting and praying their sister was delivered of the demon.

The parents were overcome with emotion. They now saw that they had been betrayed by their Chinese goddess. Overcome with guilt for what they had brought upon their daughter, they renounced their devilish worship and invited Christ into their lives. 'That night,' said Joshua, 'we were so scared by what had happened, that we all slept with our Bibles clutched tightly to our chests.' One brother held his Bible so tightly that when he awoke the next day his hand was stiff.

That was the beginning of Chinatown's KT satellite.

Many other ethnic groups

Wynne continued with his programme of developing these groups of ethnic Christians that he could see rapidly increasing in the Sunday congregations. So, realising that God was willing to give him the ideas as long as he was willing to ask and listen, he began to take steps of faith in this direction.

Around about this time Ethiopia was in political turmoil and thousands of Ethiopians fled to this country. Again, in this prayer-talk Wynne had developed with the Lord he heard God say to him, 'KT should hold out helping hands to the Ethiopians.' He knew that one Ethiopian had started attending the church so after one morning service Wynne invited him to his office. With the thought of his idea of reaching out by means of culinary evangelism, and much to the Ethiopian's astonishment, Wynne asked him, 'What do Ethiopians like to eat?' 'Curried eggs!' he said. 'All right,' said Wynne, 'next Sunday we'll have hot curried eggs after the morning service. You go and bring all the Ethiopians you can find and they can have really hot curried eggs.' Wynne told me, 'I've never drunk so much water in all my life. Those hot curried eggs were like a volcano inside me!' That's how the large Ethiopian satellite church was born. Today there is a very big Ethiopian church attached to KT.

The Caribbeans began to come in large numbers. They liked calypsos and cricket, so the church formed a cricket team and the musicians among them joined one of KT's growing number of bands. A very fine choir was established which attracted many commendations after their appearances on television and radio.

One significant approach which Wynne made at this time was to concentrate on one ethnic group at a time.

There were many reasons for this. Obviously, he could give more attention to nurse each satellite into adult life. It also allowed existing church members to adjust their attitude to the change in the style of worship that different groups brought with them.

Sadly, not all church members adjusted to these changes. 'We certainly went through hoops,' said Wynne. 'For instance, there was the time when we had an American preacher as a visiting speaker. There's a huge difference between American culture and ours. This visitor had preached five times that Sunday so when he came to the evening service, he was obviously tired. He had been on his feet a long time so they were swollen. So he took his shoes off, not discreetly, but quite openly and as he was preaching. Now we had hundreds of different cultures represented in the crowded church, and I won't mention which culture he offended, but as soon as the service finished I had a delegation waiting for me. They said, "Our folks are very upset, Pastor Wynne." "Why?" I asked. "To take off your shoes in public is an insult to our people."

'Now I can't have my members running me around, and imposing their wishes at the expense of others, so I said, "There are probably things in your culture which may offend me. But I must be prepared to make allowances. And so should you." Yes, we went through hoops but out of it came one church—KT—that accepts everybody.'

What do Filipinos like?

One day God said to Wynne, 'Did you see those Filipino girls in church yesterday? What is it that Filipinos like?' When Wynne asked them they said, 'Parties.' So they started having parties on Saturday nights. This resulted in Filipinos who were not Christians, responding to the warmth of welcome they received at KT, attending the Sunday morning services. There were so many that they began opening their own churches. Many worked in hotels and to accommodate them KT encouraged the opening of Filipino satellites in different parts of London.

My first encounter with the vibrant London Bridge fellowship, one of KT's leading Filipino churches, confirmed Wynne's vision to me. It was packed to the door. The pastor was a Filipino lady called Lily Florida. Lily, though quietly spoken, is a highly motivated bundle of energy who could have been a high flyer in the City. Before she became a Christian, Lily ran four business posts concurrently. 'But,' says Lily, 'it was just to keep myself busy. I was so fed up. However, when I got to KT I said to myself, "This is the church for me." It was full of the activity that I had been used to in business life.'

Lily had been in England since 1973, returning home in 1984. She wasn't a Christian at this time. 'I was having a miserable time,' she said. 'I was looking for peace. I was looking for love. I had tried everything. You name it, men, alcohol and more.' However, she arrived home in the Philippines to find that all fifty members of her family had accepted Christ as Saviour. She found it surprising and weird. Then two weeks before she was due to return to England, as a result of the testimony and prayers of her people, Lily also became a Christian. When her friends knew she was returning to England they told her about Kensington Temple as a church she must attend.

'In Notting Hill Gate there is a fruit stall,' said Lily. 'I was standing there when I heard singing, and it was coming from a building nearby.' It proved to be Kensington Temple! 'For me it was like a heavenly choir,' she added.

'I remember during the second Sunday I went to the kitchen and asked, "Can I do something?" The first job I was given was washing the Communion cups—and I was so happy! I really thank God for Wynne Lewis. He really has the father's heart and that's why people were drawn to KT—they felt he was a father; he has that charisma. His spirit has flowed to Colin Dye—he's the same. Of course, Colin's helped me a lot spiritually through his teaching—his seminars in the Bible School, and to grow spiritually is my personal desire.'

Lily Florida is typical of the many who have made KT their home. Later she enrolled for training in IBIOL (the International Bible Institute of London), and this prepared her for the part she was eventually to play in KT's expansion. She has opened three satellite churches in London, another in Bristol and even one in Antwerp, Belgium. The church she now pastors in West London began with only nine people, but now has two hundred.

We asked her how she managed to get her church to grow so quickly. 'The key we used at first was to form cells. This was one of the lessons I learned at IBIOL, so we grew in cells. That called for patience and persistence. From the first nine we became twelve. Then we divided our group into three. That seemed foolish to some people, but we divided to grow. We would have a Bible study followed by a meal. People responded to this very warmly. Some were added who were married to Filipinos, others were friends, and then we supplemented these activities with door-to-door evangelism.'

Lily reminded me of the month-long series of meetings arranged and led by Colin Dye with the principle aim just to wait on God. 'This was so that believers could train their spiritual hearing so that they would be ready to hear God speak to them,' said Lily. 'Then the Holy Spirit came upon the church. It was a tremendous happening. People were falling down, some being baptised in the Holy Spirit.

It was like the Day of Pentecost—we saw it with our own eyes. During that time Colin Dye wasn't touching anybody. The people were just being ministered to without human intervention. We were just witnesses of how God was moving in the church. And not only us in the church but also people outside KT in the street. Because when you get out of KT there's a bus-stop. And people standing there were open-mouthed, saying, "We thought this was a church. Why are people coming out drunk?"

'The following night people came to investigate, just to see what was happening inside. Some were saved and baptised in the Holy Spirit. We could see that God was working in the church. He was working in me as well. Nobody encouraged me to go to Kensington Temple. Nobody encouraged me to stay there. But I knew that God had led me there, and I knew I would grow in him in the church.'

A multi-cultural exercise

Wynne sought the Lord for an answer to these cultural problems and the difficulties he was encountering attracting people with different ethnic origins. So the thought came to him that the best way to attract other nationalities to KT would be for them to have fellowship with those of their home countries during the period they were acclimatising themselves to an unfamiliar environment. So he encouraged them to cook their national dishes in KT's kitchens. Having been a member of the platform party on many occasions I can testify to the tempting aromas that frequently wafted along the platform towards the end of the Sunday services. I think that is where the credit for shorter sermons should be directed!

One of the considerable and invaluable contributions to the success of KT from the ethnic groups was their tremendous emphasis on intercession, especially the Africans. Their leaders were men and women who were prominent in their home countries but had to flee because of a change in government. Men like Sam Larbe, a former major in the Ghanaian army, and now an Elim minister, has planted several churches in south London. Others had come to London to further their studies and they joined in nights of prayer. Many of the intercessors were barristers. Having come out of their countries as political refugees they were functioning in London as barristers, but their greatest function in KT was as intercessors.

An African princess becomes KT's leading prayer warrior

One of the refugees was a princess, better known as Florence Lubega. She was a descendant of a distinguished royal line and a former student of C.S. Lewis at Oxford University. As mentioned earlier, Florence held two portfolios as a Cabinet minister in the Ugandan government, alongside her husband who was Minister of Finance. This was before Idi Amin snatched power from the previous president. But Florence was also a prayer warrior par excellence! They opposed this vile dictator, which resulted in the murder of Florence's husband, and she had to flee for her life. With the help of her African servants she made her way across the border into Kenya and eventually found her way to Nairobi.

Her former Oxford tutor at St Hugh's College, Dame Marjorie Perham, who had moved to Nuffield College, Oxford as a senior don, heard of her plight. She sent sufficient money for her air fare to London. Princess Florence stayed with Dame Marjorie in Oxford for a year, but then decided that she should go to London and find a job.

But who was going to employ a Ugandan princess with an honours degree from Oxford, and with Amin on his precarious throne in Kampala still seeking revenge on her?

Just as many other African Christians arriving in London hear along the grapevine that if they want a church with an international flavour and a welcome for anyone irrespective of colour or social status, then KT is the place for them, Florence also heard and came to Kensington Temple. She found herself in the congregation one Sunday morning, and cleaning the church on the following Monday. During this time Wynne arrived to replace Eldin and Florence continued as the church cleaner earning enough to keep body and soul together. Kindred spirits usually find themselves attracted to each other, so it was that Florence met Janet Campbell who was then Deputy Director of Mencap. They had one special thing in common, a love for the Lord that was all consuming. Another was a deep-seated conviction as to the value of prayer, and I have been told by more than one person that if you want to hear someone really pray then seek out an African. Florence and Janet became prayer companions, and their burning desire was to see every seat in the Temple filled with people worshipping the Lord.

Florence and Janet covenanted to meet together at the Temple at six o'clock every evening after Janet had completed her day at the office. 'After cleaning the church,' said Florence, 'I had a wonderful time with the Lord. So instead of going to my little flat until Janet arrived I went upstairs into the church balcony which was rarely used in those days. I started praying and reading the word and then I found a change beginning to take place in my own life through doing that.'

Florence continued, 'Janet and I experienced an anointing on our prayers as we prayed for the congregation to expand. I said to Janet, "Why don't we pray that this church gets filled up?" Some people thought we were wrong in the head. I must confess that we were doing things that were not usually done.' So Florence, not content just to clean the church, also prayed. In fact, as she cleaned each chair she would lay hands on it and pray over it. Then with Janet she went into Pastor Wynne's vestry and they laid her hands on his more expansive chair. With a delightfully mischievous smile on her face she told me that one day as they were in Wynne's vestry praying in tongues and laying hands on his chair, they became aware that someone had entered the room. She opened her eyes and looked around only to find Wynne standing in the doorway with a quizzical look on his face. 'He didn't say anything,' said Florence. 'He quietly closed the door and left. But we were a bit embarrassed. We didn't expect anyone to catch us praying in the pastor's room as we laid hands on the place his bottom usually rested. We prayed, "Lord, anoint your servant to do your work in the best way possible."'

Colin has told me that he has no doubt that the success of KT in those days was as much due to the prayers of Florence and her African compatriots as any of the other reasons we now care to advance for the secret of KT's growth.

Africans and Asians have wonderfully sensitive spirits. They have the ability to get close to God and hear him speak. In the West I fear that we have been adulterated by so much of the cynicism and scepticism of the world around us. Florence, like many of her compatriots, frequently found God speaking to her through visions. One of the visions she had of KT was in 1983. She was careful to emphasise that she felt the vision was not confined to KT but also applied to the whole Church. She saw a large area covered with junk cars and rusty engines. Then she heard a voice behind her saying, 'What these engines need to save them from the destroying elements of rust is oil.' God was saying that what KT and other churches needed was the oil of the Holy Spirit.

In another vision Florence saw a large black figure entering KT and intermingling with the people as they walked into the morning service. She took this to mean an attack from satanists in the area of Notting Hill Gate. She was aware that many witches had covenanted to close KT and disrupt the family life of its members. One of the witches would walk around the Portobello Road market blowing fire out of her mouth. This was no pseudo-magical trick as seen on TV. She was an evil woman, and later, by the power of God, was to confess it. KT's young people hadn't encountered this in their evangelistic street work, so they appealed to Florence to help them. This forthright and dynamic lady, filled with the Holy Spirit, accompanied them one Saturday morning to the Portobello Road area and confronted the witch. Florence with her African background was familiar with this form of devil power. She told me that some of the satanists had even entered KT and levitated during the services.

Florence, accompanied by KT's young people, saw the woman. She stopped her in the street and prophesied that her mouth would be sealed and that she would be unable to breathe out her fire flames from that moment onwards. And that is exactly what happened. Florence told me with an impish grin, 'When the witch tried to blow fire, it just didn't come.' Then the tables were turned. Many of the satanists of Notting Hill were converted and baptised in the Temple.

She then told me of a third vision. She saw two large hands hovering over a group of praying people in the foyer of KT. This is a comparatively large area separated from the main auditorium by a glass partition and doors. It leads to a platform outside the entrance which, before extra accommodation was found, was usually packed with people who could not be accommodated in the church. In the vision she saw and heard them chattering and not listening. Then she heard God speak to her, 'When the people are too busy chattering among themselves they cannot hear my voice.'

The secret is to spend more time with God and then he begins to talk to us. Florence said, 'God said to me, "Moses was always listening to me when I was speaking to him. But these people speak so much they can't hear me speak to them!"'

Princess Florence remained at KT for fourteen years, but early in the 1990s she returned to Uganda to recover the many farm lands and buildings belonging to her family that had been impounded by Amin. Within a year, with KT's help, she began the work of restoration and a programme of evangelism to her own people. On the last occasion I saw her, she said that 2,000 had been converted and 1,000 were being prepared for water baptism. But not without opposition. Not long after she returned to her village she was confronted by an African witch-doctor who posed as a Christian minister. He would cast spells on people telling them that one of them would die on a certain date, and that their death would appear as from natural causes. After a lengthy time of prayer she received a word from the Lord, and then confronted the man. She challenged him to meet her in the village square and invited the people of the village to join her. She stood before the witch-doctor and prophesied over him. On the authority of the Spirit she told him that he would die. She then announced the time and date. And he did, and he was punctual!

'Enough barristers to keep me legally sound,' says Wynne

Recounting some of the remarkable stories of the African Christians, Wynne said that these people formed the bridge between heaven and earth. 'It is an amazing church,' Wynne told me. 'When I was there we had about 100 barristers. I was legally sound! But we also had enough doctors and nurses to staff a moderate-size hospital.'

Some people have difficulty in understanding that ethnic groups in a church should have the opportunity of meeting separately. To them this speaks of segregation. However, that is not the case at KT. When ethnic groups conduct their own meetings and in the style more familiar to them, the new arrivals from their home countries can immediately identify with them. Then after that first introduction they are more ready to join in the multi-racial meeting of the whole church. KT's leaders believe that this facility of all nations worshipping together is a vital part of the church's ministry. All three senior pastors have given special emphasis to this expression of Christian unity.

Embarrassed by numbers

KT is probably unique in church growth. The main auditorium can seat almost a thousand, if you fill every nook and corner of the nave, the transepts, the U-shaped balcony and the spacious upper and lower platforms. It was in the 1980s that the congregations began to leap upwards from hundreds to thousands. Hundreds each Sunday were being turned away because there was no room for them in the church.

This is how Wynne described his dilemma:

'We had probably started to adapt the building before

the phenomenal growth because we had no space other than the main building and a small little minor hall behind. So, along with one of the elders who was a builder, we asked ourselves, "What can we do?"

'There was only one way to go—and that was to excavate and go down. That's how the lower hall came into being which can seat about 250. Not only that, we also built offices in the space we managed to provide through rearranging the back of the church. We also modernised the entrance. But there wasn't a lot we were allowed to do with it because it's a listed building. That's an amazing story too. Eldin, my predecessor, wanted to pull the building down and replace it with a new and enlarged auditorium. However, the local residents objected, and persuaded the local government to place a restriction on the building. This meant we were not allowed to alter the outside.

'So we found ourselves in an impasse. Here's this vision I had of 5,000 people, and here's the church with only 950 people. I thought, "Lord, what do we do next?"'

'There was nowhere in Britain doing multiple services where I could go and enquire, "Look, how do I start multiple services, what are the pitfalls, the dangers?" The only places were in America where there's a totally different set of circumstances. So I put off the thought of adding a nine o'clock service in the morning for six months. In the end the Lord spoke to me. "Come on Wynne, no more waiting, off the diving board, son!" So off the diving board I jumped, and the following Sunday I announced to the eleven o'clock service that in a month's time we would be starting a nine o'clock meeting. And it was a great success? Not a bit— only eighty people turned up! Indeed for a whole year we never rose above eighty, except for special meetings.'

Wynne was disappointed at first, and began to wonder if he had made the right decision. However, there were eighty more seats available in the eleven o'clock service, and that was no problem because they were filled very quickly. So Wynne gritted his teeth and kept at it, asking the Lord what he should do.

Shortly afterwards the thought came to him that he should make the nine o'clock service different. The eleven o'clock would continue to be very lively, a great celebration, but the nine o'clock would be slower, softer and meditative. He also transferred the Communion service from the eleven o'clock to the nine o'clock service. In fact, by this time there was not enough room at eleven o'clock for the Communion Table which needed to be just in front of the platform because that space was now needed for the seating of the congregation. So any who could loosely be called 'sacramentalists' switched to the nine o'clock meeting. That probably increased the nine o'clock service by 150. Within three years there were over 700 coming to the nine o'clock service. And still the eleven o'clock was overflowing.

Wynne then started a two o'clock service. No more than seventy people came to that for the first few months. But suddenly that took off and people in the entertainment world came because they were usually late risers after their Saturday night engagements. Later, in Colin's time, a five o'clock Bible study was introduced and it is not unusual to find it attended by as many as 500 people. It lasts for one hour and is a solid period of deep Bible teaching. In these days of short attention spans it speaks of the deep hunger in the members of KT for an extensive look at the Scriptures.

Colin Dye joins Wynne Lewis

This rapid expansion both in London and abroad called for trained leaders. Wynne Lewis and KT's elders made this a matter of prayer and came to the conclusion that

KT needed its own training programme. And that is how the International Bible Institute of London came into being. It currently has 300 full-time students, with many more on evening diploma courses. The curriculum includes practical pastoral experience in KT's Pastoral Placement Programme, which offers an internship to those called to the ministry. This involves placing inexperienced leaders alongside experienced pastors whereby they learn by doing.

Many prominent people in the entertainment and sports world attend KT, and their talents are employed in IBIOL's School of Creative Ministries. This includes subjects related to drama, dance, music and singing. The Artistic Directors are Carrie and David Grant who regularly appear on BBC TV and ITV.

Soon after God spoke to Wynne on his hospital bed he gave him the vision of KT as a 'sending' church. It was a recurring thought, from which he could not escape, that he should establish an international centre from which evangelists would go all over the world. To do this Wynne realised that these 'ambassadors' of the gospel of Christ would need training. And training meant a programme. It needed someone capable of devising an educational plan. He knew there was a man who could do it—Colin Dye.

Looking back on this period when I was away from KT I can now see how God was directing the men and women he knew would be the ones to fulfil the prophecies he had given earlier concerning the future revival of Kensington Temple.

IBIOL

Colin's own development and background are described later, but for the moment it is sufficient to say that in the late 1970s Colin had been Eldin's pastoral assistant, and had then spent several years gaining leadership experience elsewhere before returning to KT in 1985.

Within twelve months of Colin's return to Kensington Temple he formed the International Bible Institute of London and received his first student. Other students followed and today an aggregate of 1,000 students are trained annually.

God not only spoke to Wynne but quite independently Colin was also given a vision. 'Early in 1986,' said Colin, 'the Lord gave me a picture of KT members receiving gifts from the Holy Spirit. These were packages of different shapes and sizes, gift-wrapped in co-ordinated paper, indicating the diversity of gifts coming from the same giver. As the packages were opened, they were found to contain saws, hammers, chisels and trowels. The Holy Spirit was reminding me that his gifts are practical tools given for the purpose of building the church. They are neither toys for amusement nor ornaments for display. However, what was most challenging,' continued Colin, 'was that although in the vision the people were overjoyed at receiving their gifts, they did not seem to know what to do with them. They needed to be trained, organised into a task force and released into the work.'

This was the basis on which Wynne and Colin founded IBIOL, and it has worked. Through this training programme KT has begun to see the fulfilment of this vision. Men and women are being trained, equipped and released into the ministry.

Reflecting on the ensuing years Colin says, 'We have found that it is not enough merely to teach and hold seminars. We must follow Jesus' discipleship training method. Simply imparting factual information produces students who know a lot about the kingdom of God, but are not discipled into doing its work. Jesus' methods were similar to our modern system of apprenticeship, in which the experienced tutor passes on his practical knowledge and skill. The trainer acts as the model giving verbal explanation as he goes along. Then the apprentice works under supervision until he is fully trained. Finally, he is able to pass on his skills to others.'

The 'Joshua' principle of the Pastoral Placement Programme

Colin continued, 'Wherever appropriate, we provide this kind of on-the-job training in addition to classroom lectures, discussions and seminars. Jesus' approach certainly proved effective. After Christ's ascension followed by the coming of the Holy Spirit, the disciples were equipped to preach the gospel, heal the sick, cast out demons and raise the dead. They had learned to minister like Jesus.'

It is estimated that by the end of this millennium there will be more than 3 billion people living in cities worldwide. London is one of the principal cities in this array. It is not only rich and diverse in culture but populated by people from almost every nation under the sun. A walk down the West End's Oxford Street gives emphasis to this fact as you may traverse the entire length of more than a mile and not hear a word of English. Kensington Temple, one of the largest churches in the UK, is at the centre of this great metropolis with almost 200 satellite churches reaching into London's suburbs, and these include numerous ethnic groups. (Colin Dye decided to give a more appropriate name for this grouping of charismatic churches, fellowships and ministries which now number some 400. It is now known as 'The London City Church based at Kensington Temple and the Tabernacle at North Acton' where IBIOL is now located).

The Institute offers a unique place for practical training from large city-wide celebrations at the London Tabernacle at North Acton, Wembley Arena and large London halls, such as the Royal Albert Hall, to small local outreaches. Colin's ambition is to win London for Christ and push back the evil that spreads its poisoned talons from the cesspit in Soho. Soho may have the best restaurants but it also has the filthiest hovels where wicked men and women exploit the sexual fantasies of the emotionally vulnerable.

People from every nation on earth make their home in London and its environs. What a mission field; what a place to train for ministry!

There were other interesting developments, even amusing ones. The Chinese people love getting up early in the morning, so they came to the 9 am service. But the Africans liked the 11 am service—they are usually slow starters. Many of them would wander in at 11.30, so Wynne began to warn them: 'The day will come when you'll wander in at 11.30 and you'll find we don't have any seats for you.' And of course it happened. One Sunday there was chaos. The latecomers had to stand on the steps outside. However, the next Sunday they were half an hour early!

A Director of Social Services

The church leadership began to recognise that in the mass of people now attending KT there were many with broken hearts and broken lives. Wynne began to wait on God for his direction in the field of counselling and practical help. Just at this time Ruth-Ann Cannings appeared on the scene. She had come to the UK from her home country which was then British Guyana to become a qualified nurse. Ruth-Ann enjoyed her work in London's hospitals, and it soon became obvious to those around her that she was gifted in her 'one-to-one' work with patients.

In 1973 the renowned concert cellist, Jacqueline du Pré, was admitted as a patient to St Mary's Hospital where Ruth-Ann was nursing. Jacqueline was in the advanced stages of multiple sclerosis and needed special nursing. Soon Jacqueline and Ruth-Ann became very attached to each other. 'She gave me the name "Smiley",' said Ruth-Ann. This was very significant because Jacqueline's experience of nurses had been an unhappy one.

Very often Jacqueline would apologise to Ruth-Ann for the trouble her physical condition would cause. But Ruth-Ann was quick to put her at ease, saying, 'This wouldn't be happening if you could help it, would it?' Reassured, they turned painful situations into a smile. 'We laughed a lot,' says Ruth-Ann. After that, if Ruth-Ann was on duty she was the nurse that would respond to Jacqueline's bell. Fellow nurses would say, "She wants you, Ruth-Ann."

A year later and after Jacqueline du Pré had left hospital, Ruth-Ann met her at one of her huband's (the famous conductor Daniel Barenboim) concerts. Ruth-Ann once again also met Jacqueline's family. The concert came to its conclusion and Ruth-Ann began to leave. Suddenly she felt somebody grab her by the elbow. It was Daniel's mother. 'Would you come and nurse Jacqueline?' she asked. Somewhat taken aback, Ruth-Ann asked for time to think about it. After a great deal of reflection and prayer, at the end of two weeks she took a step of faith and accepted Mrs Barenboim's invitation. 'I knew it was the right thing to do,' said Ruth-Ann. 'I was there twelve years nursing Jacqueline and even running the home. I can honestly say, even though Jacqueline's last days were extremely painful, I have no regrets. I have proved that if God places you some place he gives you the ability to stay there.'

Jacqueline was a very special lady. The same person who played the cello with such vitality and great fun was also a person who desperately needed to be cared for. Her playing was an extension of her personality. Ruth-Ann recognised in those days in the hospital that what Jacqueline needed most, was more than just nursing. She needed constant reassurance that she was loved as a person, not just idolised as a famous concert cellist. In a BBC radio broadcast Jackie's sister, Hilary, talked to Libby Purves about Jacqueline's final days. She said, 'Ruth-Ann was Jackie's nurse. She was wonderful. Extraordinary. Jackie's last years were wonderful because of Ruth-Ann.'

Listening to Ruth-Ann tell her story we could see that not only was her caring companionship for Jacqueline of inestimable value to this talented lady, but it was also a time of preparation for Ruth-Ann for work that she was later called to undertake at Kensington Temple.

After Jacqueline's death, Ruth-Ann was almost traumatised with grief. She suffered a period of painful disorientation. Wynne Lewis and his wife, Carol, comforted her. They even took her on one of their overseas preaching tours. This opened up an opportunity for her to use another of her gifts, her beautiful singing voice.

One day, much later, Wynne said, 'I want to see you in my office.' 'Help! What have I done?' she thought. He then told her that the members of his Church Board comprising seven men (they were usually referred to as 'The Pentagon') had been concerned about a gap in KT's ministry. Many in the congregation had left their homes to live in London, and were in need of a one-to-one encounter. Wynne and his board had been praying for someone who could set up a pastoral care division. Ruth-Ann's name was put forward for prayer. So it was decided to offer her the post of Director for Pastoral Care. She was flabbergasted. 'Either you're crazy or I've got jet lag!' (She had just flown in from a visit to the USA and was planning to return there.) 'I'm a nurse—I don't know anything about being a director. What's more, I hate desks!' she replied. He sat her down and said, 'Ruth Ann, I'm not crazy—you may have jet lag. But I know that these men would never have made this decision lightly.'

David Shaw, one of the church elders, was leading a prayer meeting at the time and as Ruth-Ann slipped into one of the back seats of the church hall, he was reading from the Song of Solomon. Suddenly she heard him say very clearly, 'Come my beloved, come unto me.' 'I really felt those words were addressed directly to me,' said Ruth-Ann. Then she had an experience she had never had before. 'I couldn't think,' she told us. 'My thinking capacity just went. And in that blankness I clearly heard the Lord say, "Service or not. And if it's not, I can never use you again with the same anointing."' So she responded quite simply, 'Service,' and went back to Wynne's office that very night and to his astonishment announced, 'The answer is "Yes, I don't seem to have a choice."' She slammed the door and left before he could say another word.

Wynne, in his customary style, just pushed her in at the deep end. Within three months she had formed a pastoral care division. Somebody said, 'Ruth Ann, you've been a nurse, you've taken care of Jacqueline. You have managing skills because you ended up managing the home and managing people. Even hiring and firing the household staff.' Then the penny dropped. She was going to be working for KT full time. 'Lord, what am I doing here?' she asked God. She was astonished to hear him say, 'I want you to wash my disciples' feet.'

She saw her work as caring for people. At first it was mainly the staff. To this day a staff member will come in and maybe have a cup of coffee, then talk about something that is bothering him or her. She just had to wash their feet and send them off. Then it was not just the staff, but anyone who was in need. Ruth-Ann really felt God just lifted the level of compassion that she already had as a nurse to a spiritual level.

KT now has an extensive 'social concern' programme staffed by a fully trained team of counsellors. These counsellors (who include lawyers and medics who offer their services free of charge) give advice on employment, housing, legal matters and medical problems. Running alongside this social programme is a 'spiritual concern' programme with its weekly 'healing clinic'. This allows time to deal in depth not only with physical illness but also the 'inner hurts' where the root cause is frequently found. Every weekday pastors are on duty in KT between the hours of 9.30 am and 5.30 pm offering a personal counselling service, including advice for those contemplating marriage. They also give personal instruction on parental responsibilities for those who request that their children should be dedicated. Meetings are also designed specifically for youth. These include a crèche for toddlers: junior church for the four to eleven year olds; and events for teenagers.

One of the essential qualities of a good leader is the ability to see the potential in people and then help them to develop their capabilities. All three of KT's senior pastors have had this gift. Indeed they continue to use it in their present responsibilities. Wynne always stood on his 'observation platform' as KT began to grow, because growth carries with it extra responsibility. No longer can church business be compared to a small village shop. It is more like a big business operation in the city high street. You can imagine the heavy financial responsibility that rests on Colin Dye's shoulders as KT's annual turnover runs into millions. So how can the pastor be expected to 'care for the coins' and be the 'curé of souls' at the same time in so vast an organisation?

'Kemi Ajayi arrives

In 1990 Wynne and Colin found the right person to take 'care of the coins'. 'Kemi Ajayi had worked at the Nigerian High Commission and afterwards as a research assistant at MARC Europe, the Christian organisation responsible for statistics about the Church in the UK and its many organisations. 'Kemi had come to London with her husband who had been appointed to a diplomatic post at the Commonwealth Secretariat.

So what was 'Kemi's first impression of KT? 'I was arrested by the ability of Pastor Wynne to turn things round very quickly,' said 'Kemi. 'Kensington Temple appears to have the ability to attract workaholics! I don't think I know of anyone on the staff who is not a workaholic.' She soon discovered that it's that energy that keeps KT expanding. 'Wynne's vision to win souls for Christ and plant churches was like a magnet to my husband and me.'

'Kemi used her considerable skills to organise the many departments of KT, and when they were complete and running she felt God calling her to explore the possibility of opening satellite churches specifically for French-speaking people. During her research work she discovered that the highest concentration of French speakers in London was in the Notting Hill District. They had come from various nations. In KT alone there are over sixteen nationalities who use French as a first language, France, Switzerland, Belgium, the Mauritius, the French West Indies, Canada, West and Central Africa among them. In addition she discovered that as a result of the political situation along

Africa's Ivory Coast and in Zaire, vast numbers of political refugees had flooded into London.

So it was probably not a coincidence that at one of the 'Christians in Sports' meetings at KT someone should ask her if she knew anyone who was French. It so happened that there was a French family in KT who spoke very little English. Matters came to a head for this family when the son ran into serious problems. They needed help. 'Kemi, who is fluent in French, said she would meet them. When she did, she was surprised to discover that their knowledge of the Bible and Christian teaching was very limited. They didn't even know how to pray. So she counselled them, ending with a prayer. Following that meeting 'Kemi began looking for a French-speaking church where they could continue to receive spiritual help, but without success. This really troubled her. Here were infant Christians in a strange land with very limited knowledge of the Scriptures. They had not been taught to study the word of God, so 'Kemi wondered how they could exist spiritually, let alone make any progress. She was only too well aware that being a Christian in a foreign country is an uphill task. 'I know God is there to help,' said 'Kemi, 'but one also needs to know what to do and these people didn't know what to do.

'I believe the Lord used this family to really challenge me. My first university degree was in French. It was on that basis that I got together with a few other French speakers in KT and shared with them the vision of opening French-speaking churches under the umbrella of KT. I also shared it with Colin. He encouraged me to prepare a plan. So I began with a meeting for French people only on the level of fellowship at first, because I was still fully occupied as Director of Finance and Administration for the Temple. However, a year later we actually launched our first French-speaking church.

'Our mission is to reach the Francophones in London with the gospel. We aim to reach people with influence, not just making converts. Of course, we want to make converts, but we want converts who can also make converts. Our aim is to plant churches that can plant churches. There are now two in London and one in Paris. We also have others: ten in the Francophone zone, with another four to be launched by the time this book is published.'

One of 'Kemi's Bayswater satellite house-group leaders has a group of about eighteen people. They meet regularly on a Saturday. 'Kemi is now in the process of training this leader to become a pastor, so he has enrolled in KT's Apprenticeship Programme. This is a programme of training so that on completion the graduates become pastors and start their own Francophone assembly. One group, mainly comprising people from the Congo, already meet separately from other French-speaking Christians. This may seem strange. But the fact is that the way they worship, pray and sing is so different from other French-speaking believers that they find themselves more comfortable in meetings under their own control. Even in Africa there is no one group that can be described as 'typically African' or 'typically anything'! KT is about making the gospel available to people in a way that is relevant to them. Eldin, Wynne and Colin soon discovered that it was unwise to try and impose any form or style of worship with which a group, cell or satellite was not comfortable.

Many Christians who have come to KT from other countries have done so because of the harsh and dangerous conditions in their homelands. Sometimes their families are still being hounded by the authorities of their home countries. In one of KT's satellite congregations both husband and wife had been involved in their country's politics. The wife had been in prison and brutally tortured. She had to escape on foot to another country, eventually arriving in England. The situation in their home country then changed, and the husband decided that he should return to continue his work in the political life of their homeland. In the three years he had attended the KT Francophone satellite he wonderfully matured as a Christian. Although all the details cannot be revealed at this stage, 'Kemi has been in the process of ministering spiritually to someone who is potentially head of state in that country. This prominent leader and his family have already made a commitment to Christ.

Do you sell Braz food?

KT is made up of many fascinating stories, and it would take a big book, a very big book, to do justice to them all. In 1990 a young married couple arrived in London from Brazil. Enoch Pereira with his wife, Anna, had planned to go to Africa as missionaries, but they first needed to speak English so they came to London to learn the language. Then, like so many others, Enoch heard of Kensington Temple. He met Colin Dye. He enrolled as a student in IBIOL. And now he speaks English as well as Spanish and his native Portuguese.

Enoch is a man who cannot exist doing just one job alone. So he decided to open a Portuguese-speaking church in London. And how do you find Brazilians in London? The answer he found was the one God gave to Wynne Lewis. Food! Brazilian food is sold in Latimer Road which is part of North Kensington, just a stone's throw from KT. Brazilians like food, their own kind of food. And Braz food is what Enoch and his helpers serve after their Sunday morning services.

Enoch not only visited eating places where Brazilians gather (there are 20,000 Brazilians in London) but the places where they play football. Brazilians are football mad. The wizard of the football field is Brazil's world-famous Pelé. So Enoch went to Hyde Park and joined his fellow countrymen playing an *ad hoc* game of football. Soon five of them came to the Latimer Community Centre (Brazilians have bad feelings about the use of the word 'church'), and accepted Christ. He noticed one young man wearing the jersey of a well-known football team in Rio de Janeiro, 'Flamenco'. He was in London studying English as part of the qualification he needed to be an airline pilot back in Brazil. Enoch befriended him and said, 'Would you like some Braz food, and drink a Guarana (a fruit drink) in our community centre?' He readily agreed, then stayed on for the evening meeting. To Enoch's astonished delight that young man gave his life to Christ that first night. Later he married one of the girls of the church, and now they are back in Brazil where he is an airline pilot.

Enoch has opened ten churches in the London area, as well as Portuguese-speaking churches in Frankfurt, Dusseldorf, Munich, Hamburg, Stuttgart, Amsterdam, Rotterdam, Paris and Brussels. He also has plans to open churches/community centres in Vienna, Oslo, Copenhagen, Madrid, Rome, Antwerp and Athens. His goal is 100 of these satellites linked with KT and many of them receiving KT services via their satellite dishes. He didn't get to Africa in the way he first envisaged, but now he has twelve churches in Mozambique where plans are well under way to open a Bible school with dormitory accommodation. This is also designed to provide conference facilities for potential leaders from distant parts of the country. What a happy bunch of people they are at his community centre at Latimer Road!

I was caught up in their uninhibited style of worship when I went there to preach.

One day a medical doctor from Morocco arrived at Enoch's flat in Latimer Road. He was in trouble and needed to see a priest, and someone gave him a leaflet with the Latimer Road address. Enoch says that God must have a sense of humour because although the doctor could speak eight different languages, he couldn't speak Portuguese. However, that did not deter Enoch, and using the limited English he then possessed he told him about Jesus. The doctor was a Muslim, but soon he was captivated by the message of Jesus. One day he arrived and said, 'I want Jesus in my life.' He then wanted to return to the Middle East to tell his family and friends about his new life with Christ, and after attending a training course at All Nations Bible College in Hertfordshire he returned home as a WEC missionary. There he met a medical doctor, who had also left her home in Switzerland to share the Christian message with Muslims.

'I was preaching in one of the largest churches in Malaysia one Easter a few years ago,' Wynne told us. 'They have about 4,000 people in the congregation, and the senior pastor asked me if I recognised the young man on the platform who was leading the singing. I told the pastor that I couldn't place him. Then he told me something which confirmed our decision to set up the International Bible Institute at KT. "He was saved, baptised in water and in the Holy Spirit when he was in London and attending KT. He was then trained in your Bible Institute, and now he's on the staff here." This young man later went on to plant a church in Melbourne, Australia where he's doing exceedingly well.'

In their world travels, Eldin, Wynne and Colin frequently meet leaders not only in the churches but in national governments who became Christians at KT during their stay in London. People who are now significant in politics and commerce such as Kwako Boeteng, father of Paul Boeteng, a minister in Tony Blair's government, was an elder in KT before returning to a prominent place in Ghana where he had previously been a cabinet minister. Presidents and ambassadors of several African countries attend KT's Sunday services when visiting London, so it's not unusual to see cars with diplomatic corps insignia bringing African presidents, accompanied by their bodyguards, to Sunday morning services.

Hyde Park is just a few minutes walk from KT and there at 'Speakers Corner' KT's budding preachers undergo some gruelling experiences as they preach in the face of a barrage of heckling from the sceptics in the crowds. IBIOL is not a 'hideaway' from real life to study ancient philosophies, but a training unit in the heart of hostile country. Its prospectus offers 'training at the cutting edge'. Students come from a wide range of backgrounds which include housewives, graduates, dancers, businessmen, architects, designers, nurses, cooks, mechanics and many others. Actors and entertainers, sportsmen and women take time off to better themselves spiritually, and even pastors and teachers arrive for refresher courses. 'Insight' days are frequently held for teams of ministers from other countries to see and hear at first hand what is happening in a large busy city.

The curriculum is designed to cover enough subjects to provide training on three levels: 1) general discipleship, 2) methods for those wishing to improve their skills as leaders, 3) the Pastoral Placement Programme. This is a full-time programme lasting for one year during which equal emphasis is given to study and practical 'on-the-job' training. In fact this has been copied by many old-established theological colleges.

KT spreads towards France

One other place of special interest to Colin Dye is the cultural and spiritual centre of the Francophone world, Paris. Sadly this city has been steeped in secularism for hundreds of years. From a worldly point of view its majestic boulevards, colourful cafés and grand architecture make it one of the most beautiful and vibrant cities in Europe. However, Colin believes that France is on the verge of emerging from this spiritual wilderness. People are beginning to hunger for truth. He says, 'We believe that God is ready to visit this nation in all his power and glory.' KT wants to be there when it happens and contribute to this Holy Spirit revival. KT now has a church in Paris which, as described earlier, is under the oversight of Dr 'Kemi Ajayi.

On the same pattern as in London the church in Paris has its own training institute, the International Bible Training Institute of Paris. It is also designed to serve other countries on the European continent. The course combines faith-building and relevant teaching with practical 'on-the-job' training and is geared to enable students to discover and minister in their callings while growing in experience in all fields of ministry.

The fact that one thing leads to another is common enough, and that is how KT has grown. Arising from its interest in other countries, the need for its own language school was the next development. And so ISOL (International School of Languages) was opened. Its purpose is to provide language tuition in English for students of non-English speaking countries. In keeping with KT's international vision of also reaching countries in Africa, Asia and Latin America, other languages are being added to the curriculum. At present classes are offered in French, Arabic, Portuguese and Spanish. IBIOL also offers tuition in Hebrew and Greek, and there is even also a course in Deaf Sign language.

Part-time courses are also offered by IBIOL during the evenings. Mondays: The Word—a course which includes surveys of the Old and New Testament and the principles of understanding the Bible plus a survey of Christian doctrine. Tuesday: The Leader—this covers leadership awareness and skills, preaching, church planting and counselling. Thursday: Evangelism—a course that includes teaching on such subjects as intercession, spiritual gifts, healing and world missions.

School of creative ministries

The arts are particularly important to Colin Dye. He was keen to establish a good arts department so he set plans in motion for a School of Creative Ministries. This is presently headed up by Peter Hutchinson who is supported by the talented husband and wife team, Carrie and David Grant. Carrie and David are well known in the entertainment industry. The overall object is to maximise the talents of such Christians in the arts and media. As the great authority on communication in a modern age, Max McLean, says, 'Creative men and women are in the Church. Some express their art through music, the only art fully accepted by the Church. But others sit quietly alone; waiting to be affirmed, encouraged, supported. They are waiting for the body of Christ to understand and find room for the novel, the film, the play, the masterpiece ruminating within, that could reach beyond the subculture and challenge the basic assumptions of our secular age and point the world toward the ultimate truth.'

Carrie and David Grant are singers and actors who regularly appear on BBC TV programmes such as *Top of the Pops*, and ITV. Carrie was a presenter for several of ITV's West of England programmes. She and David entertain in clubs and theatres, appear in plays and are highly sought after soloists and duettists.

In one of her engagements she met another girl singer with whom she had worked on *Top of the Pops*. Carrie knew very little about Christianity at the time, and what she did know appeared unattractive. However, her friend had become a Christian and the change in her life had a profound effect on Carrie.

'At the time I was on a big search,' said Carrie. 'I was looking at Buddhism and spiritism.' Then Carrie met David when he was guest soloist on one of her TV shows, and he started talking to her about Christianity. This was somewhat unusual for him because he was a lapsed Christian. The other 'co-incidence' was that he was friendly with Carrie's friend, Boo Beggs (her stage name) and her singer husband. Boo had 'found' KT and had led hundreds of people to Christ. 'A fantastic woman,' says Carrie. 'Jesus' was the main subject of her conversation and she soon talked to Carrie about him. It was not long before Carrie attended a Bible study meeting at Boo's house and as a result she committed her life to Christ. That was followed by David's return to Christ.

Carrie told us, 'Boo was just so wonderful. I just could not believe the change in her, and that made the biggest impression on me. She just seemed to have so much love as she talked to me about Jesus. I thought, this is the truth, this is what I've been looking for. I relate to this love, and I relate to the truth of it—it just hit me so squarely.' On the following Sunday (7 November 1986) Carrie found she had a little bit of time before leaving for Newcastle where she was to record one of the shows in her TV series. She happened to mention this to Boo. Quick off the mark Boo said, 'You must come to my church, Kensington Temple.' It sounded a bit Hindu and weird to Carrie, but it appealed to her at the time! So she went to KT. She arrived alone and sat downstairs. As she looked around at the rows and rows of all kinds of people in this crowded church, she said to herself, 'This is amazing.' There were so many different colours and cultures—'It was brilliant.' Boo saw her and quickly came down to fetch her. 'We all hang out upstairs, come on up.' There was a completely different atmosphere upstairs,' Carrie said. 'All the trendies seemed to hang out up there! So I went upstairs and it was just brilliant.'

What impressed Carrie was the singing and the lively atmosphere. 'I'd never heard anything like it. As a singer, I thought it was beautiful. I just thought, I can't believe these people—they look so in love. But they were all in love with Jesus! I'd only seen love like this when one of my girlfriends had met a new man! But they seemed to be doing it to God. Then the other thing that hit me was that the preacher didn't wear any clerical costume. I thought that when you went to church it was all very 'thees' and thous'; a place where everyone wore costumes.' But she found they were dressed like others, just suits. Her impression was that this church was so different. I went there and I loved it. Everything that comes out of KT is done in a very dramatic way, but it's not just a performance.' She was to discover that this is the way the gospel is presented at KT, and it appealed to her. It was so professional. It was something she did not expect, but warmed to because she was used to it in the entertainment world. But here she was in a church!

Then Boo began to tell her more. 'Well, this is what we do in this church, we tithe.' So the very first week Carrie tithed. Then Boo said, 'No sex before marriage.' So Carrie said, 'OK. That's it. No more sex.' Looking back on those days, Carrie believes that her stable Christian life now was the result of the way she was discipled in such a brilliant way. Everything that she heard Boo say, the church backed up. They were not afraid of touching on these personal issues.

David's roots were far removed from Carrie. He had been raised in a devout Christian family which meant he not only knew his Bible, he had even been a Sunday-school teacher. However, he had let his faith slip as he climbed the ladder of success in the entertainment world. But he was still dissatisfied with a life estranged from God. Now he found himself in love with this gorgeous and beautiful girl called Carrie.

'Hey, you'll never guess what, there's this fantastic church I've been to, and they're all singing really loudly,' Carrie told David. But David wasn't so sure. 'Well, I don't know if I agree with that,' was his rather superior response. So the next week she took him along to KT. He very cautiously walked alongside her as they climbed the steps into the Temple. 'Right, well I'm sitting at the back,' he said. And in the back they sat. In fact it was the very top row at the back of the balcony. 'You cannot get further away than that,' said Carrie. 'You feel like you're on another planet!' For the first half of the service David just sat there with his arms folded. She glanced at him. 'I don't know if I like this,' he said out of the corner of his mouth. 'I don't know whether I can agree with this.'

But as the meeting progressed, she noticed that he began to change. As he listened to Wynne Lewis preach, he was muttering to himself, 'This man's fantastic.' Then somewhat cautiously he thought Wynne was rather irreverent. Wynne made people laugh, and David hadn't been brought up to believe it was proper for people to laugh in church. In the strict church his family attended that wasn't done. People around him were wearing short sleeves—and no ties! The women didn't even have hats. It was a culture shock, even for a man in show business. But by the end of the service, the change in David was about complete. What Wynne preached was biblical, and David's family were very strong 'in the Word'. The service lasted two hours! And neither Carrie nor David were bored!

'I took to KT just like a fish to water,' said Carrie. 'I think it depends on your conversion.' It took David a little longer to adapt to this new way of Christianity. Whereas for Carrie 'it was black, white, thunder, lightning—really incredible. One day I was going in one direction, the next day I was completely changed. At that point I think God could have asked me to do anything and I'd have done it.'

Carrie and David, now married and blessed with a delightful young daughter, decided to put God first in their lives. They continue in their careers, singing and acting, producing and directing, which is where they believe God can best use them. They use their talents to train others at KT's School of Creative Ministries. 'He changed us but he didn't change our work.'

One of the main things that God has placed on their hearts is to bring the arts into the gospel world and then to take those arts into the market-place. There's no such thing as 'I'm a gospel singer and you're a secular singer'. We're singers! So one day they'll be doing *Top of the Pops* on BBC TV, and the next day they'll be leading worship in KT or one of its many satellites.

'David and I felt that it was really important, as artists

who are Christians, to take with us the next generation of young gifted Christians out into the world, or wherever they want to go with the Christian message.' The day after giving us this interview David and Carrie were scheduled to perform in the BBC's young people's programme, *Blue Peter*. In their music band they have three of the students from KT's School of Creative Ministries.

Carrie and David can open doors for KT's young talent to perform with leading artists. And what artists they are! Diana Ross, Garry Barlow, *Nine to One*, and *Top of the Pops*. Recently when they were rehearsing for *Top of the Pops* with a well-known artist, in between 'takes' they were singing Christian songs. Their fellow artists hearing this unusual sound came to their dressing room and asked, 'Can we come in and just listen?' 'That's our witness,' they say. 'We stand in places where you wouldn't hear Jesus praised. When the curious come, they often ask for prayer. We have fantastic times.' It makes things much easier for them to have a former member of the Royal Ballet as their pastor, Colin Dye, because he understands.

Around 1988, Peter Hutchinson was working on a Thames TV soap opera called *Gems* when one of the girls on the same set asked him if he would like to accompany her to Kensington Temple. Peter had never heard of KT, and when she went on to say that it was the church she attended, he became very dubious. However, he was curious that this girl should find a church that interesting, so he went with her. After the service he met two other actors, Caroline and her husband Greg, and they just started talking about Jesus. 'I wondered what I was doing in this mad building,' said Peter. 'I'd been aware of "happy clappy" churches before but hadn't been to one. In the acting profession one tends to beware of such places, but I hadn't bargained for a church like KT.'

Like Carrie and David, Peter found himself in the balcony and was similarly amazed and uplifted by the singing. 'I responded to the singing and the electric atmosphere. I certainly felt that sense of theatre, and it really lifted me in some inexplicable way.' Just as others had found, especially those who had not previously encountered a KT-type meeting, he was impressed by the sense of freedom. And the people! They were all so involved in all that was taking place.

Peter had studied at the London Academy of Music and Dramatic Art for two and a half years before joining the Phoenix Theatre Company in Leicester. Afterwards he came down to London and employed an agent. Then good things started happening and he was appearing on TV, in theatre and films. But for some unknown reason to him then, he grew restless. Now he can recognise that this was the time when he was being made ready to hear the call of Jesus. Soon it happened in one of KT's evening services.

Colin Dye was a great encouragement to Peter. He invited him to enrol in KT's Joshua Programme. David and Carrie had set up KT's School of Creative Studies and they invited Peter to join the teaching staff. However, their commitments in their professional life prevented them giving all the time the School needed, so it followed that Peter became its Director. To assist him was the bubbling, effervescent Jumoké, a night-club jazz singer and presently presenter of one of London's highly successful BBC radio chat shows.

So what is Peter's philosophy for the School? 'I hope that believers can come and develop their creative gifts within a conducive Christian environment. After their period of study we can release them and disciple them on to the next stage in their creative career.'

All over the world, Christians are rising to the challenge of reaching a media-oriented unchurched generation, and the School of Creative Ministries is designed to do this. The course covers key foundations in the area of Christian character, philosophy of creative arts, drama and singing. The intention of KT's leaders is that this ministry should not be confined to London. The plan is to give it a world-wide ministry by becoming an inspiration to peoples of many lands.

KT's influence was now reaching out to those in the entertainment world—not the easiest of areas to reach people with the Christian message. This is compounded by the unsociable hours such people are required to work. Peter now plans to start a TV and video production course in the next curriculum year. Satellite TV is now an integral part of KT's evangelistic outreach.

But not everyone has to be a talented singer or actor. 'One girl, from Croydon, came to us for an audition. I said, "Why are you here? You can't act or sing. What do you want?" Then she talked to us about her idea for a theatre company, so we took her in for training. That was three years ago. She now has a gifted group of people working within churches in Croydon, producing and presenting the Christian message in drama. She's taking them into schools, working in the church, in the community, on the street.'

Peter's wife, Karen, had arrived in KT a couple of years earlier. Her parents were Christians but during her teen-age years she had drifted away from anything Christian. In fact, she began using drugs when still at school, even-tually becoming a dealer. Soon she was mingling with some of the important families of the day, even supplying drugs to the sons and daughters of the aristocracy. But her ambition was to be a successful actress. 'Although I earned a lot, I never seemed to have much money,' Karen recalled. It seemed to disappear as fast as it came as a result of her 'extravagant life-style and drug habit'. When the police seized a boat-load of drugs in the Bristol Channel things began to get too close for comfort, so she moved to London where she opened a fashion shop. But through all this time she could not find the satisfaction she thought that going to parties, posh restaurants and wearing fashionable clothes would provide. She had taken a flat which happened to be close to KT and it was there on her own that Karen says she had a real encounter with the Holy Spirit'.

Then she met Wynne Lewis! That meeting was to change the whole course of her life. She was visiting her parents in Bristol when Wynne walked in. Here again Wynne's sensitive instinct came into play. Recognising that this lady was spiritually hungry, he invited her to attend one of KT's services, promising her that she could be in for a surprise. He assured her that it was not the conventional type of church. She accepted his invitation, little realising that she would soon be enrolled as one of the first students of IBIOL with Colin Dye as her tutor. Attending KT's many activities she encountered several people with similar backgrounds and history with whom she could empathise, and this made her feel secure. This was effective because they knew she spoke from experience and not a text book.

Another chapter in KT's life now came to an end. To the surprise of many, Wynne Lewis accepted a call to the leadership of the Elim churches worldwide. But God had his new man for Kensington Temple, Colin Dye.

Colin
Dye

Within a short space of time, Colin Dye had risen from one of the young people in one of the country's largest churches to become its senior minister.

Colin was born in Kenya in 1953 in the middle of the Mau-Mau uprising which meant that he knew about danger from his earliest days. However, his father decided to take the family to neighbouring Tanzania which was also more convenient for his business affairs. Early in life Colin showed a propensity for ballet and after the family made a further move, this time to Australia, he began to take it seriously and joined the Western Australia Junior Ballet Company.

He soon attracted the attention of leading choreographers and much ahead of his time he was given principal parts in *Giselle* and *Les Sylphides* partnering senior ballerinas. He was inspired by the leader of the Company, who was of Russian descent, who encouraged him to make ballet his career. To further his ambition he came to London and gained a place with the Royal Ballet Company. Here he eventually got his first big break with the lead part in *Giselle*. But he had not encountered Christ or his message. This was to change with the arrival on holiday of his brother from South Africa. He belonged to a Pentecostal assembly. It was natural for Colin's brother to share with him the joy of his faith in Christ, and before the holiday was over Colin had committed his life to Christ. As his brother left to return to South Africa he impressed on Colin the need for a good spiritual home, preferably a Pentecostal assembly.

'So I came to KT. What an experience!' recalls Colin.

'I can remember my first visit very clearly. That would have been around March or April 1971. I was baptised about six weeks later by Eldin Corsie. In my book on prayer I described my first reaction to KT in the same way as "a duck takes to water". In another sense it was like coming home. It was friendly, and I liked the style of worship which, way back then, was nothing as robust or as loud as it is today.'

This was over twenty-five years ago. Even so it was much more exuberant than the other churches he had visited in the Kensington area. Also, the congregation felt *big*. (Here again it was small in comparison to what it is today). Nevertheless, in his bones he felt that KT was destined for a great future. People were being saved every week. Today he sees that time as one of destiny, although he would not have been able to articulate it as such. What he was soon to discover was that his search for a fulfilled life was over now that he had encountered Christ.

'It's strange,' says Colin. 'I've studied philosophy since then, and I can now see that I must have been a bit of an existentialist.' As he progressed in his Christian experience he began to realise that his dancing had been part of a spiritual search. He had been looking for meaning, something to live for.

In its own way his conversion was very dramatic. Even though he couldn't put it into words, he already began to feel a sense of calling. 'I knew in my heart that I was going to serve God in some full-time capacity.' During his time at the Royal Ballet Company he would bring with him several of his fellow dancers to the services. It was quite a sight, Eldin told me, to see a whole row of dancers in the body of the church. Eldin was also good at discovering new talent and soon found a job for Colin. Today's congregations will be surprised to read that this involved cleaning the wash-rooms and the passageways in the basement! 'Now isn't that amazing of God. He tests our servant spirit,' says Colin. God knew that this young man was not averse to doing dirty jobs. After that Colin went to work in the church office before serving as a deacon, then as an elder and finally an assistant minister to Eldin. Although this appeared to happen by accident, it is a common practice in some large business companies to insist that their future managers should first pass through all the stages of the company so that they will experience first hand what it is like to work in all the departments they will eventually have under their control. Colin then attended a two-year course at a theological college in Cambridge where he met his wife, the lovely and talented Amanda. Amanda now takes a very active part in KT's life, and to hark back to Dr Boreham's description of the value of his wife, Amanda is a true 'makeweight' to Colin.

Following college he returned to KT and Eldin arranged for him to work in a drug rehabilitation centre whose director was John Harris, another member of KT's pastoral team.

This is how Colin describes the unexpected work experience which was to prepare him for future ministry at KT: 'I saw the inside of the drug scene in London. It was an incredibly important learning time for me. But coming out of that, there was no chance for preaching. It was practical service. I didn't despise it, it was street work, practical service, clearing up after drug addicts, all kinds of stuff. It gave me a tremendous feeling for the practical area of service in Christian ministry. There was also a grounding experience in prayer, evangelism and reaching out to deprived people. That sounds condescending, but they were needy people. To put it another way, people that other churches were not bothering with.'

Eldin had recognised that Colin was a potential church leader. As Lyndon Bowring had departed to head up Elim's evangelisation programme for Greater London, Eldin enlisted Colin as his pastoral assistant. It was a small leadership team at that time, the latter end of the seventies. Eldin and Colin were full-time workers. Eldin was constantly praying; he was talking about revival, talking about the church being filled—and believing God for this church to be filled. He was in constant prayer for God to come and revive the church and for the miraculous to be restored in a way that hadn't been seen in the past. He had been part of a healing evangelistic band himself when he was a young minister. He used to be the pianist for many evangelistic crusades, so he had a strong evangelistic and visionary emphasis.

When Wynne arrived at KT, Colin continued as associate minister. But Wynne, as he says, had other ideas for Colin. Wynne says he gently nudged him out of KT to gain experience as a pastor with sole responsibility for a church. Colin was appointed pastor of the Elim church in Winton, Bournemouth. He was there for four years, and he was beginning to think that he had been abandoned and that he was destined for life 'in the sticks'. But that was far from God's thoughts. By one of the happy 'coincidences' of God's planning, Colin undertook the arduous task of taking an extension course in Divinity with London University. Just after Colin had completed his university course, gaining the Bachelor of Divinity degree, he received his call to return to Kensington Temple. He responded to Wynne's invitation (not without some understandable hesitation) and in 1985 he returned to be one of Wynne's associate pastors.

Though Colin is a successful pastor and a gifted preacher, his one great passion is prayer. He has said on more than one occasion, and in my hearing, that of all the ministerial gifts God has given him, the one he treasures most is prayer.

How has Colin planned KT's prayer programme? 'I think the best way to answer this is to say that I have sought to develop an ethos of prayer and an environment of prayer so that even before people think about what they are doing, they are automatically praying about it,' says Colin. 'I think that the example of this is the Notting Hill Carnival where we have seen huge differences and real change taking place. I think the overall climate and atmosphere of growth is as a result of prayer.

'I have built prayer on two basic principles. First of all, the senior leadership must accept full responsibility and not delegate it. They are the intercessors. I am the preacher, they are the pray-ers. Of course I get people to pray for me, but if something is going to be prioritised, the senior leadership has to be involved and be right up front leading, so that it is a major thing. That is probably the key factor.

'When we come together for corporate prayer, we hardly ever see it as an end in itself. We see it as lighting a fuse. It is more like a briefing session. It is setting the tone of prayer. It is setting the direction of prayer, and

raising the issues that need to be prayed about. We are
touching on them and praying them through. We then
commission people to go back to their homes, to their
groups and pray them out. So actually in that way you get
a week of prayer; you get a continuous prayer meeting
until you return for the next prayer meeting.'

One of Colin's acts, early in his ministry as Senior
Pastor, was to establish a prayer division. He had the right
person on hand to lead it.

KT's Prayer Director

Some are called by God to be evangelists, but everyone
should evangelise. Some are called by God to be intercessors, but everyone should pray. I have a friend who has
been called by God to separate himself to live a life of
meditation and prayer. He is a Franciscan friar and lives
alone in a hermitage. But not all of us should be like
Brother Ramon.

June Freudenberg knew from early in her Christian life
that prayer was to be her ministry. But in direct contrast
to Brother Ramon she finds herself mingling with the
crowds. She is involved in every aspect of KT's ministry,
because they all need prayer support.

June was born in Australia and for the first part of her
life worked there and in New Zealand. Then she came to
London, and in 1988 she joined the staff of KT as its
administrator. 'But,' said June, 'I didn't see myself as an
administrator although I liked organising. So I didn't
think for one minute it was going to be permanent because
the Lord had spoken to me when I was seventeen years old
to encourage people to pray.' After eighteen months in
administration she opened her heart to Wynne and Colin,
and told of her teenage call. When they asked what she felt

she should do, she said, 'I don't know, but whatever it is it has to be with prayer.' And that, after many stages, is what June does at KT. She is its Prayer Director.

'My work is not a platform ministry. It's teaching, training, leading prayer meetings. I am responsible for keeping KT's prayer antennae fully extended.' It is to make sure that everything is covered in prayer. Her duty is that of facilitator.

June has seen KT develop under three different ministries: the strategising, the multiplying of the cell groups and satellite links. 'If you took away the satellites and cell groups we would just be a church,' she says.

Then there's the Wednesday night prayer meeting—a great intercession time when 800 people fill the church. The team here shares the burden of the church's vision with the people, and they join in praying it through. KT is a place where people are not just hearers—sermon tasters—but doers.

Colin decided to restructure the Wednesday evening meetings. The first thing he did was to put the prayer meeting back into the hands of the senior leadership. Then he rearranged the whole day. The staff met early in the morning for prayer. During these prayer times the staff were invited to list those subjects for prayer that they felt God was placing on their hearts and minds.

Then Colin shut himself in his office for the whole of the afternoon in earnest prayer. Sometimes he would break off and call in members of staff to shed further light on their department's activities, and any difficulties they had encountered. He would even telephone people in the city asking them to share their thoughts for prayer. 'We allowed the Spirit to lead us in everything,' he said. 'From the first time we did this our church prayer meeting came alive as never before.' No longer were people arriving late for the prayer meeting just in time for the Bible study that followed. No longer were members seeking out pastors for counselling when the prayer meetings were in progress. Everyone had to be at the prayer meeting. The numbers attending the prayer meetings leapt into the hundreds and soon the main church was filled to capacity.

With such numbers, how can everybody pray? Colin explains, 'We pray in unison. Everybody prays together. Some people are going to be intimidated by the size of the building with the result that you get the same courageous few praying each week. Then there is the danger that that will limit the number of prayers. Some people may even become bored with the repetitions. So we use what we sometimes call the 'Korean style' or 'African style' of public praying. People stand up and pray together. Not in a haphazard way, praying as they see fit, but given a sense of direction from the leader. The leader will say, "Here is an issue—here is how we are going to pray." Then the whole congregation prays, and the timid ones are not worried about the sound of their voices because they are part of the whole. We sometimes call this method a prayer concert.

'I think this is how they prayed in the early Church. Acts 4 says that after Peter and John were freed from prison "all the believers united as they lifted their voices in prayer" (v.24, NLT). Yet the writer, Luke, was able to summarise verbatim what they prayed. He could summarise it because that was the content of their prayer. Everybody prayed. They all prayed together. There seems to be a biblical precedent for that in the way their prayers were multiplied. Another way we adopt is to divide the congregation into small groups. People can then pray audibly and in turn without feeling intimidated.

'The other thing we try to do is to teach people that there are many modes of prayer. The Africans are very good at aggressive spiritual warfare. They bring their hand grenades to the meal table and blast the devil even when they are saying "grace". We have learnt a lot from African believers in this way. But also, believe it or not, we invite the people to spend some of the time in silence and contemplation. There are times when we need to listen to what the Holy Spirit is saying.'

Listening to Colin giving those thoughts on prayer, I was reminded of some words of one of his associate pastors, Enoch Pereira. 'We have to have balance,' said Enoch. 'What I see in Christian circles today is that people get a word from God and then rush off to act upon it. They don't wait for that word to be in season. So we need to know the times and season of God. We have to have spiritual understanding. If we don't have that we make mistakes. I have learned to hear from God and then wait for his time to act.'

'We feel that the combination of prayer and prophetic ministry is very strategic,' continued Colin. 'Prophetic praying is important. But the way I see this developing is for people to see that praying alone is not enough. We also encourage people to combine their praying with practical things, so that it is not just praying for people in need but also making an effort to go out and minister to those needs. It is faith and works. Prayer is never on its own in the Bible. It is prayer plus action. We feel that action has got to be seen more in the community because it is one thing to be praying in a closed building for the community, but we must also make ourselves visible in the community. We must be ready not only to pray but, for example, to visit people with AIDS, those who are lonely, sick and passing through hard times.'

The Watchmen/Watchwomen

June Freudenberg is also responsible for running the Watchmen programme. Those who make a pledge to join the Watchmen programme are asked to make two promises. The first seems obvious. Prayer has to be priority number one. The second is probably harder. Certainly, as a Watchman myself, I find it so. They must pray for one hour at a set time each week. The Watchmen are fed with topics for prayer by June. There are 1,000 KT members who have committed themselves to this programme.

I found two of the many operations of the Watchmen particularly exciting. The first involved an imaginative use of modern communications. Prayer teams were assembled at KT and then they made their separate ways to different parts of the city. Remaining at base was a large prayer group, and this group was in constant radio contact with the prayer teams as they traversed selected areas of London. As the teams sensed the spiritual needs of the areas of London through which they passed they radioed the relevant information back to KT headquarters. In some cases the atmosphere of evil was so strong that they had to call on KT to join them in co-operative prayer.

The second operation was to hire a river launch on the River Thames. A team of KT's Watchmen engaged in earnest prayer as the launch passed places of national influence such as the Houses of Parliament. The boat travelled by the City of London between the bridges of Blackfriars and the Tower of London. They prayed for the West End as it cruised under Waterloo bridge. Theatreland is close by. Colin, with his memories of his days with the Royal Ballet Company, was only too aware of their need for prayer.

The Fishermen and Fisherwomen!

Colin says that as soon as he had the Watchmen in place the Lord showed him the next step. It was in the words of Jesus to his disciples, 'Come, follow me, and I will make you fishers of men.' This is mentioned in Mark's Gospel. So the Watchmen were followed by the Fishermen. The terminology is sometimes a problem for some people. Shouldn't it be Watchwomen and Fisherwomen as well? Of course.

KT's youth teams are also active in London's West End. They have been led by a refreshingly enthusiastic young man called Kristian Lythe. Kristian comes from the North-east of England. He was only eighteen when he came to London after a somewhat rumbustious early life. One day in his mid-teens he 'found' God. 'I used to listen to a lot of tapes on my Walkman,' he said. 'I listened to a lot of preachers talking about revival. When they described the Holy Spirit moving across Britain I felt the presence of God all the time.

'One day I went straight from work to my friend's house for a prayer meeting. We were seeing visions and God was showing me a lot of things. Every day at work God would minister to me as I listened to these tapes.' One of the tapes prompted him to leave the North and travel to London. It was there he found Kensington Temple and became a student in KT's IBIOL.

'For the first six months I was getting distinction after distinction. Then in the February I started doing evangelism which slowed down my college work. But I was on fire for God and wanted to evangelise all the time. The whole of the first year was great—it was the grounding in the faith that I needed. Before I came to Bible school I never really knew who I was as a Christian. If you asked me what I believed I probably wouldn't be able to tell you, but at Bible school they were teaching me great Bible truths. I said, "Yes, I believe that. I agree with that." It grounded me in my faith so when someone asks me now I can say, "This is what I believe."

'I was pretty bored one Saturday night, and went to see one of my friends. I suggested that we went to Leicester Square. When we got there, there was a crowd of Muslims shouting at a group of Christians who were conducting an open-air meeting. The Muslims then started debating with us. I had about five Muslims around me. Although I didn't know much about Islam I was declaring that Jesus is Lord.

'Then I read a book by Yonggi Cho about prayer being the key to revival, and my friends and I started praying. One day we were all quiet before God when suddenly the power of God hit me. I fell on my knees before him. It was as though he had ripped out my heart and put his heart in me. Soon everybody was really crying to God for the lost.

Evangelism in theatreland

'The following Saturday we returned to Leicester Square but this time double the number responded to the gospel, including a lot of young people from overseas. Many were broken-hearted. They had messed-up lives and some were homeless. Ever since we started praying earnestly we have found God beginning to bless us. We really attacked the enemy with violent prayer, declaring that Jesus is Lord.

'One night we prayed with much passion because we knew we needed the power of God. We held hands and cried out for the fire of God to fall. After about two hours I couldn't stand up any longer. I was so aware of the presence of Jesus. It was totally supernatural. We started to speak in tongues and found we were speaking the same language. It was as if we were having a conversation in tongues. After similar energising experiences we would go to the Square at about eleven o'clock on a Saturday night and stay there witnessing to passers-by until about five in the morning.'

Kristian told us that 'between one and two thousand people have been saved on the streets' around Leicester Square since they started this street evangelism. The critical question is 'Where are they now?' In honesty he confessed, 'I don't know. But we've got a book of names and addresses. Of course, it's hard to keep in contact with all of them because most of them return to their home countries.' It appears that half of the converts were from overseas. However, Kristian and his friends now have about 700 names and addresses and they have written to everyone. They also planted a KT satellite in nearby Covent Garden led by one of the pastors of KT.

'The new believers want Jesus but they don't want to go to church,' said Kristian. 'So in our Covent Garden meetings it's mostly singing worship songs. We just blast the worship out! We're passionate about God. We jump and dance and sing. They do it in the nearby night-clubs so why shouldn't we do it, but unto the Lord? Why shouldn't we also jump and dance and sing for Jesus? We have a party and dance and sing.'

Kristian and his friends then erected a satellite dish. Now Colin's preaching at KT can be seen and heard in Covent Garden. They meet in a restaurant called the Mongolian Barbecue. It is a mission field after all. And In line with Wynne's culinary evangelism they have food as well!

KT is always expanding

It's quite common for a church to suffer a fall in attendance when the senior pastor leaves. This was thought likely to happen when Wynne left KT to become General Superintendent of the Elim Church. In fact the opposite took place. When Colin assumed full responsibility as Senior Pastor he led the church in his own way. Before long it was found impossible to accommodate all those who wanted to attend the Sunday morning congregations, even using all the ancillary rooms. So a search began for a suitable hall nearby. A 700-seater hall was found in the Porchester Conference Centre in Queensway, just a mile away. Arrangements were then made to install a microwave dish so that the second service could be received. But soon even that was not enough and two other halls have now been added with similar relay facilities. The secret of their success is that each hall has its own pastor. He conducts the opening part of the service before taking a feed from KT containing Colin's sermon.

This could well be the pattern for the future of the London City Church as already there are some twenty similar relays across London. Experimental broadcasts are also being made to halls in Paris and Brussels. More than 10,000 people are now attending the London City Church and KT's services, and the numbers continue to grow. There are over 300 'Care' or cell groups (kind of mini-churches), as well as ethnic churches where weekly services are conducted in French, Spanish, Portuguese, Cantonese, Arabic, Tagalog and Amharic. Many KT members attend these ethnic satellite churches because they do not as yet speak sufficient English to benefit from the main services. A remarkable feature of this expansion is that KT has found the world coming to its doors—a veritable mission field.

There is a department for world missions sending teams (at their own expense) to many countries on the continent of Africa, Latin America, throughout Asia and several European countries. This is under the oversight of Philip Whitehead. Philip was trained as a teacher, and found himself with an increasing love and concern for Africa. He worked on missions in Africa for four months, and there the Africans encouraged him to go to KT on his return. They love African missions, they said. So he did.

Colin is not slow to enlist someone he recognises as a potential leader, and persuaded Philip to enrol in IBIOL. This resulted in him working under Gareth Lewis, Wynne's son, on world missions. He has now taken teams of KT youth to pioneer in Albania, South America and his beloved Africa. During a mission in Africa's Voodoo country, the Republic of Benin, so many miracles took place that these occult-ridden people recognised a greater power and thousands turned to Christ. 'You preach a different Jesus,' they said. 'You preach that Jesus is here now. Not just a historical figure. He's alive with us now.'

'I must tell you a story about Benin,' said Philip, 'just to show you the sovereignty of God in that nation. We chose that nation for a mission just after the fall of communism. We had no contact, so we went there without anyone preparing the way for us, but we were sure God wanted us to go there.' The man who was the leader of the communists had been ousted. But while he was out of power he heard the gospel and gave his life to Christ. At the time the Government was under the control of Voodoo witch-doctors. Colin accompanied Philip and the KT team on the mission and prophesied that there would be a change of Government. Later when Colin met the converted communist, he told Colin that he planned to run for government again. Within eighteen months the Government fell and this man was chosen to be the new President. There have been many attempts on this man's life but so far he has been kept safe. Realising that he may not always have the opportunity of speaking about Jesus, whenever he now makes a political speech he invariably ends it with a gospel message.

I wanted to become like him—so I became a Christian

In 1988 an unknown Japanese woman became a Christian without having heard of Jesus Christ. In spite of this, her dedication to the Christian way of life led her to seek out people in Britain who had suffered indescribable cruelty at the hands of her fellow countrymen and women. She began a programme of reconciliation for the Far East Prisoners of War, and that is the astonishing story of Keiko. This is how she described what happened.

In 1969 Keiko married an Englishman, Paul Holmes, whom she met at university in Tokyo. 'He was so humble, and so kind to other people,' she said. 'He put other people first. After I married him I was very surprised that he was so kind to me. I found his good points— one thing after another as we went on living. I thought he was so different that I just wondered why. So I thought it must be the God he believed in. And I wanted to become a Christian because of that—because I wanted to become like him. So I became a Christian without knowing Jesus.'

But that wasn't to remain that way for long. She learned that her husband was the sort of man he was because of what Christ had done in his life. Then tragedy struck her. Her husband was killed in an air crash. 'It was my darkest time,' she said, 'but Jesus brought me through. I said at the time, I didn't think I could go on. I said to Jesus that I didn't want to go on. Then he said to me, "My grace is sufficient for you." And I really knew it was true. He said, "We will work together." I didn't know what he meant at the time. But when I visited the Far East Prisoners of War Association in London's Barbican Centre I knew what my mission in life was to be. The reconciliation of POWs with their cruel Japanese taskmasters.

'God also spoke to me that day at the Barbican Centre at the POW conference. It was there God wanted to show me the pains, agony and frustration of the people around me. He wanted to tell me that someone has to do something. I heard him say, "It's you, Keiko, I want you to do it".'

However, as one newspaper report of the time said, 'Within seconds of Keiko's arrival at the Barbican reunion, the devout Christian from Leyburn Gardens, Croydon was the target of open hostility being asked to leave by several incensed veterans.' But Keiko was not so easily discouraged. Eighteen years earlier when she visited the small Japanese town of Iruka, just six miles from where she was brought up, she was shown the simple memorial which had been set up by the Japanese villagers in honour of the sixteen British POWs who died working at the local copper mine. Over the years the wooden crosses had been replaced by stone monuments paid for and lovingly tended by the villagers. She took photographs of the little cemetery, and in her very gentle way she began to show them to the POWs and the families of those who had died at Iruka.

In 1995 Keiko took her story to KT, and with the typical warmth of Colin Dye and his team, she was given full endorsement for her mission. Every August a special service is held at the Temple in connection with her work. Each year she raises finance from Japanese business houses to cover the travel costs of former POWs who travel with her to Iruka. The hurts and wounds of the war years are being healed. POW Jesse Adams writes, 'In 1992, with Keiko and a party of "Iruka Boys" as she has named us, I returned to Japan and went back to Iruka after forty-seven years. Seeing for the first time the memorial in the place which is now called "A Little Britain" was for me the proof that all that I had heard and read about was really true. It was at that moment and all through the days of our pilgrimage when my bitterness finally melted away. It was during that trip that I met Mr Taoka, a former guard in the Iruka prison camp, and from our first handshake he was to become the first of my now many pen-friends in Japan.'

The highlight of this painstaking pilgrimage of Keiko occurred in 1997 when she accompanied the Japanese Ambassador to the UK to be present at the Armistice memorial service in Coventry Cathedral.

Did not our Lord say, 'Blessed are the peacemakers?'

What is meant by a 'prophetic church'?

This is a strong feature of Colin Dye's ministry. He has taken on Wynne's mantle. Here are two examples.

At a recent Sunday morning meeting Colin was compelled to put aside the sermon notes he had prepared to preach. He then proceeded to say that during his prayer time early that morning, he had been listening to what Jesus wanted him to say. The Lord then spoke to him. Colin talked to the people from his heart, and in short passages. These he interspersed with a devotional chorus allowing him to contain the emotion he felt. The hushed atmosphere in the church was so intense you felt it could be cut with a knife. He told the people that he had a vision of Jesus early that morning, and he saw him weeping. Colin asked him, 'Why are you weeping, Lord?' And Jesus replied, 'People are not listening to what I am saying. I died for them. I've talked to them, but still their lives are unchanged. They are not listening to what I'm saying.' Like the prophets of old, the hurt Colin was feeling was obvious to the congregation. It was etched on his face.

On another occasion Colin came to the platform on a Sunday morning to speak of an encounter he had had with Christ in the early hours of that morning.

'I come to you with this word,' he said. 'God has met with me today, and he has laid this burden heavily on my heart. I feel Christians in this nation, and even the rest of Europe, need to grow up in the Spirit. We need to enter a totally different dimension of spiritual understanding, of spiritual effectiveness to engage in spiritual warfare. We have got to wake up. We cannot afford to lose any more men or women of God.'

The previous week the well-known leader in the charismatic movement, Bob Gordon, had died after a short illness.

'I see the church in Britain as ill equipped for battle. But God has given me good news for you—that is going to change. I have this message from God for you and it is how we can silence the enemy, the "avenger". (Phil. 3:16). Many of us know how to break through in the Spirit, but it is not enough to break through, we have to learn to *maintain what we attain*. In other words, we must not only break through, but we must keep hold of the ground that we have gained. God not only wants you to get on top, he wants you to stay on top. God is saying to me that he wants us to go from vision into reality. If we're not careful we soon buy into this defeatist philosophy. New levels, new devils. Haven't you heard that Jesus has the victory?

'It is not how big you are or how big you become, it is how big God is that counts. It is out of your mouth that strength or praise comes. Here is a word for you from the Psalms, "Out of the mouth of babes and infants you have ordained strength . . . that you may silence the enemy and the avenger" (Psalm 8, NKJV).

'Now here is the revelation. It's not complicated but profound. We do not know how to fight on both these fronts. We only know how to do one and not the other, and that is why the evil one can pick off men and women of God like ducks on a showground. It has got to stop. We've got to rise up. We need to know what it is to silence the enemy. God has given you authority. And this is what it sounds like: "Enemy, shut up!" You can't be nice with the devil. Silence the enemy! It is not enough to know how to silence the enemy—you also have to know how to silence the "avenger".

'Maintain what you attain! When I saw that in the Spirit it broke my heart because I know it applies to me. We are experts at letting revelation slip away. I saw in the Spirit that the '"avenger" is an even more vicious spirit than the enemy. The "avenger" belongs to the heavy mob. When you have a spiritual victory in your life, and you have a successful breakthrough in some area of your life destroying some aspect of the enemy's activity, that is only a fraction of the battle. The greater battle lies ahead, because the spirit of the "avenger" is a vicious spirit, far more vicious than even the initial spirit-opponent that you were facing.'

Using an Old Testament story to illustrate the point he wanted to make, Colin said, 'After you have defeated

Ahab, watch out! Jezebel's coming. Elijah was a prophet raised up for one purpose, and that was to destroy the spirit of Baal. A pagan, demonic worship. The real source of this demonic power was Jezebel the queen. Ahab, the enemy, was no more than a puppet in the hand of Jezebel, the "avenger". Elijah challenged Ahab and the prophets of Baal on Mount Carmel. He said, "The God who answers by fire, let him be God." And the fire came and consumed the sacrifice and the nation fell on its face before God and cried out, "The Lord he is God." That is the victory. The story would have been so different if Elijah knew what I'm about to tell you.'

Colin then went on to explain: 'It's not arrogance when I say that. I have the whole story. Elijah didn't have it. What happened next was that all the prophets of Baal were destroyed. When Jezebel heard this news she issued orders for Elijah's execution. She was the spirit of the "avenger". Our God shows us how to silence the enemy and the "avenger". He has ordained strength for both sides of the battle.'

Colin then continued with this word of encouragement from the Lord for the people of KT. 'We will not turn back. We will rise up and destroy the spirit of Jezebel, the spirit of the "avenger". If Elijah had understood Psalm 8:2 he would have said, "You tell that woman Jezebel that by my God whom I serve, she is next to be destroyed." We can say something that Elijah could never say, "Greater is he who is in us, than he that is in the world." Instead Elijah allowed the spirit of the "avenger" to get him. The spirit of death and destruction.'

Colin then went on to give the people this strong word of assurance. 'You can break through into new levels of the Spirit without fear of the heavier attacks that come from the heavy mob. But what you need to know is that you must spend even more time with the Lord after the victory than you did before. That's what Elijah failed to do. He gave everything at first. He was then utterly exhausted. That was right in part, but afterwards he was weakened. His big mistake was that he cut himself off from the 7,000 other prophets who had not bowed the knee to Baal. Elijah was not alone, but he had forgotten that. One at a time the enemy can pick us off, but when we stand together as the body of Christ we become invincible.'

Then Colin concluded: 'Hear me well. It is time to rise up and pray for the protection of the Spirit for your leaders as never before. Do not be fooled by the anointing. The anointing is not the person. The anointing is God on the person. The body of Christ needs to wake up and rise to the point where we hold a defensive line in the Spirit through which the enemy can never break. This we can do because we understand the importance of what to do the morning after the victory of the night before.

'The spiritual climate in Britain and Europe is changing. Here in London there is a tremendous opportunity for people to explore religious beliefs. People are talking about God and the world's likely future now more than ever before. The spiritual atmosphere is conducive to people being open. There are signs of them searching for an answer. But we have to get in there with the gospel quickly.

'I think we've seen changes in the past ten to fifteen years in Britain that bring us much closer to the conditions in developing nations. The old systems have failed. People realise that there's more to life than what they've been taught. The old values of rationalism have gone. People are beginning to realise that there's a dimension beyond themselves. Young people are ready to hear.'

We have been hearing of unusual happenings in churches in Canada, Toronto; in USA, Pensacola. These have caused some people to look for similar supernatural manifestations to take place in their own churches. But this can be misleading, says Colin. 'Revival is much more than that. It's when the Christian Church wakes up to who we really are and behaves accordingly. It's when the mobilisation of ordinary Christians to do the work of Jesus Christ takes place. The Bible talks about the Church being the body of Christ. And the body of Christ is the means by which Jesus himself operates. That seems to me to be one of the key revolutionary truths that come out in revival where individual Christians join together as the body to do what Jesus calls them to do.'

Must we then expect the same phenomena to occur in Britain as in Canada and the USA? 'I've looked at this in some detail,' says Colin. 'In times of revival there's a heightened awareness of religious experience. Yes, there are often many signs, phenomena, often miraculous signs on those occasions. But they are not necessarily the essence of revival. They can be the fruit of revival. But we must beware because in some instances they can even be distractions, so they must be kept in proper perspective. Biblical revival is about Christians finding a fresh relationship with the Lord Jesus and then moving out to share that relationship effectively with others.'

Sing and make music

Kensington Temple's music is special. It always has been. Eldin Corsie is a fine musician in his own right. I know no one to equal him in sensing the direction of the Spirit in a meeting, then introducing appropriate music. KT has also been favoured by the breadth and length of the musical talent that has come its way. Perhaps the outstanding feature of today's Director of Music, Richard Lewis, is the prophetic insight he demonstrates in his leadership and the music he is inspired to compose. Like some of the hymn writers of old, he will compose sacred songs to give support to the topic of the service.

Richard is no ordinary musician. He is an accomplished concert pianist having studied music for six years both at Cambridge and London's Trinity College. 'I wanted to be a concert pianist,' he told us. 'I was not madly keen on the academic side—I was more into performance. It was normal for me to practise three to four hours every day.' Then a physical injury got in the way. He was in a Schubert competition in Germany (Schubert was one of his passions) and practising hard when he was stricken by severe pain in his right arm. This put an end to his concert career. So here he found himself, a highly accomplished pianist, but unable to endure the rigours of punishing concert tours. He was also a brilliant composer. For some years he had been a keen Christian but he didn't feel drawn towards participating in church music. By this time he had met Joy, his wife, and they prayed together to discover God's plan for them. Then suddenly it all changed for him. He walked into Kensington Temple!

'Every time I walked into KT I'd get goose pimples all over me,' he remembers. He wondered, 'What's going on here? This is very strange.' Just at this time KT placed an advertisement in *Update*, the church magazine, announcing a vacancy for a Director of Music. 'I think I ought to do something about this,' he thought. So he tentatively put his name forward to Colin saying, 'I'm a classical musician but I am willing to give it a try' Today Richard is responsible for KT's complete music programme, including a choir. He is also in charge of at least 150 people who are involved in various ways with music at KT.

One of the astonishing developments that emerged following his appointment as KT's Director of Music has been his prophetic compositions. 'It's quite extraordinary,' he said. 'When we were having the September '94 meetings, I was waiting upon God. Then I found myself beginning to write songs. One day as I was waiting on the Lord in my flat in London I was hit by the Holy Spirit. I was knocked flat in my flat with this holy laughter! After that I wrote about ten songs—just like a flow—some were written in half an hour. Then one night I woke up dreaming a song. I went back to sleep, but not for long because the Holy Spirit clearly spoke to me. "If you get out of bed I'll give you another song," he said. So I got out of bed and the words and music for "Latter Rain" came. It was finished in half an hour. I was crying my eyes out. I thought, "I've never written a song like this before."'

Richard has given me permission to include the words and music of the song 'These are the days of the Latter Rain (Not by might)' at the end of the book. This song includes the theme of Colin's book *Building a City Church*.

'Very often I'll be working on a song, and Colin will be working on a sermon. And I'll say to him, "What's your theme, Colin?" And he'll say, "Spiritual warfare." And that was the theme of the song I had been working on. About spiritual weapons of warfare. Quite uncanny.' KT has a special role to play in this country. For Richard, KT is like a big well (and he has written a song about it), or a waterfall. Just as it says in Scripture, 'Deep calls to deep at the thunder of your waterfalls.' 'KT,' he says, 'is like a revival flow which has been opened up by much prayer and intercession. This is the result of the prayers of many saints.'

The London City Church Tabernacle

One of the great steps forward in the life of Kensington Temple has been the acquisition of a much larger building in North Acton. It is called The London City Church Tabernacle. It can accommodate 4,000 people which has allowed the Sunday evening celebrations to more than double in size. Additional space is also available for the IBIOL and KT's administrative offices. However, this is only part of the vision. The name 'Tabernacle' was chosen with this in mind: it presents a picture of KT on the move. 'And it shows that we are not focusing on the building,' says Colin. 'We believe that the KT building in Notting Hill Gate is very important.'

There is no doubt that the building has been especially blessed of God, so Colin and his team are determined that it will continue to figure prominently in the future plans of the London City Church. Colin further adds, 'It's very strategic, but it's too small to do everything we need to do. In 1985 when I came back to KT from Bournemouth, the church was already too small to keep the congregations. That's why we added the nine o'clock Sunday morning service. We wondered how we could continue to grow when the building was already being filled several times on a Sunday. Now that we have moved the Sunday evening celebration from the Temple to the Tabernacle it also shows that we are not limiting ourselves to any one building.' As the tabernacle of the Israelites was destined to represent a people on the move to the Promised Land, so the London City Church Tabernacle announces to the world that 'it's our intention to follow the glory of God wherever the glory of God leads us'.

The other thing the acquisition of the North Acton building did was to signal a complete change in thinking.

This may not have been so readily recognisable in the Temple building, because KT as a building became so much a focus on its name, Kensington Temple. On the other hand the Tabernacle has not replaced Kensington Temple. The morning services are still at KT which is the heart of the London City Church. But the evening congregation at North Acton allows for the gathering of the KT family from all over London, enabling the network to come together.

As Colin said early in this story, Kensington Temple, the Horbury Chapel that was, is evidence of God's covenant with the Christians of Kensington who, in 1848, laid the foundation stone to mark the beginning of God's plan for Kensington, and through Kensington, London, and through London, the UK, and through the UK, the whole world!

The Tabernacle is only a few minutes' train ride from the Temple and it was only found after a long search and many trials. It was built about ten years ago for the BBC as a scenery and property construction unit. It must be more than just a coincidence that it should have features that will be a great asset when KT's broadcasting plans are put into full operation. It has extra ventilation and lighting systems that are necessary for high-level scenic painting, so it comes exceptionally well equipped. It has an enormous capacity: the major auditorium alone has 4,000 square metres.

Colin Dye says in his book *Building a City Church* that he believes we are on the threshold of a great outpouring of the Holy Spirit, and that we must be prepared if our cities are to be won for Christ. So what kind of church will be able to handle this outpouring? 'It is my firm conviction,' says Colin, 'that God will raise up a new phenomenon in the British churches, and to see it happen we are going to have to drop some of our old ideas of church life. We must make room for new concepts which are consistent with what God is doing today. Our cities will never be won by small, inward-looking parochial churches with a "village" mentality. We must see the raising up of vast city churches reaching across entire metropolitan conurbations. These churches will have the spiritual authority necessary to challenge the spiritual powers holding captive the populations of our cities.'

Some people frown on the idea of megachurches, but large city churches were the pattern in the days of the early Church. As Canon Michael Green writes in his book *Evangelism in the Early Church*:

> Paul's strategy was urban. He made for the centres. The Acts of the Apostles records his visit to city after city of importance. Antioch, the third city in the Roman Empire; Philippi, the Roman colonies; Thessalonica, the principal metropolis of Macedonia; Corinth, the capital of Greece under Roman administration; Paphos, the centre of Roman rule in Cyprus; Ephesus, the principal city of the province of Asia. It is hard to escape the conclusion that this succession of cities . . . was not hit on by accident. It was part of a definite plan for planting the good news in key positions throughout the Empire. The climax of his urban policy was Rome.

Furthermore, some of Rome's prominent citizens became Christians and were ardent supporters of Paul and his missionary work.

To accommodate these large numbers the early Church operated on at least three different levels. There were the small groups meeting in people's homes as we read in Acts 2: 'They broke bread in their homes and ate together with glad and sincere hearts.' Then they would meet in larger groups in some of the big houses belonging to the wealthy. Here they would receive visiting apostles and teachers who would instruct them in matters of doctrine. Finally, there would be the large celebrations. On the Day of Pentecost Luke tells us that thousands were added to the Church. Modern church growth analysts would describe these levels of church fellowship as cell, congregation and celebration meetings.

Colin's vision for KT's place in the twenty-first century is to establish a city-wide presence. When that is accomplished it will become a strong base to further develop the Temple's international ministry, thereby fulfilling the commission that Jesus gave first to Wynne and then Colin. It will also serve as a platform of influence in both the City of London, with its powerful international finance houses, and the Government and ecclesiastical centres in Westminster. The Apostle Paul always gave his main attention to the principal cities of his world. The highways built with Rome's military and economic power became communication routes for the gospel throughout the Roman Empire.

Colin's desire is 'that by the end of the year 2000 we will be fully functioning as a City Church. By that I mean a network of 2,000 churches, groups or ministries across London, capable of impacting the whole city with the gospel in word and deed. I want people to be able to feel the presence of the Church of Jesus making a difference to how things work, making London a better place to be in. I also hope we will be capable of reaching out into the 10°40° window [see p. 191]—that is, to all the nations in this band.'

KT's elder at large

Earlier in this story I introduced to you my friend Victor. He was a highly successful Arab businessman who came to KT soon after his conversion, and began a ministry to the Middle Eastern peoples in the 10°40° band, even long before this imaginative title was given to it. Victor is occasionally called upon by the United Nations to serve as an interpreter in their various international meetings. This now brings him into close contact with world leaders and gives him an entry to 'restricted-access' nations. 'Discretion is the better part of valour' is a wise old saying, and this has to be Victor's guiding rule. The best stories about his work cannot be told. But I asked Victor to describe the way he shared his Christian faith with others.

'The Lord has been working in my life to look at people through *his* eyes. As I searched the Scriptures to see how Jesus looked at people, I could see that he looked at the world as people. He called himself the "Son of Man", emphasising his humanity. He ministered to the people around him, his friends and family; to the people who loved him and hated him. He even ministered to his enemies, the Roman soldiers. His world was a "people's world".'

Victor decided to follow the way his Lord related to people. So he prayed, 'Lord, help me to make my world a people's world too.' He now meets with people at the highest executive level, and he talks to them in the terms of their, and his, humanity. Jesus had come for sinners, and Victor tells them that they are fellow sinners, just like him. Jesus looked at people without being influenced by their position, class or colour. He looked beyond external appearances. He looked right into them as human beings. This was highlighted for Victor in a somewhat humorous way when he was being briefed by the personal assistant of the president of a European country. The president's P.A. said, 'Be sure that when you shake hands with our president you don't touch his elbow.' 'Certainly,' said

Victor, 'but can you tell me why?' 'Well,' he replied, 'he's ticklish!' That certainly emphasised his humanity.

On one occasion when he was interpreting for an Arab prince, Victor asked him, 'How would you like me to address you?' 'Just by my first name,' the prince replied. Victor then added, 'Your Highness, I want to tell you at the outset that I don't want anything from you. I am not seeking to be involved with you in business. I don't want your money. I want nothing from you. As a matter of fact, I want to leave you with a gift. The gift of friendship.' At that moment Victor noticed that the prince's eyes became misty, and he said, 'Never in my life has anybody come to me to give me something. Instead, they have always come to me to take something.'

So, whether Victor meets a prince or a pauper, he invariably begins by asking him such questions as: 'Do you ever feel thirsty?' or, 'Do you ever feel lonely?' Then as the person responds, Victor will say, 'So do I.' In this way he can share his humanity. He doesn't look at the person as a Muslim, for example, but as a human being. 'That enables me to reach people at the highest level,' says Victor.

Victor and Maha also have a weekly radio ministry to the Arab-speaking world. They talk extensively about family issues and what the Bible teaches about marriage. Thousands of listeners write in for counselling. They also produce and present their own TV programmes by satellite which reach out to the whole Arab world. These weekly programmes have a potential viewing audience of over 100 million people in the Middle East.

On one of Victor's journeys to a restricted-access country he was stopped by armed soldiers and taken under guard to their army headquarters. He was interrogated by the army commander for two hours. But Victor wasn't slow to use this opportunity to present the Christian message to these men. He offered the commander a copy of the New Testament in Arabic. To the astonishment of his driver, an unbeliever, not only did the commanding officer accept the New Testament, but also his officers who were standing around him. What was an even greater surprise to both the driver and Victor, the commander then ordered a group of soldiers to accompany them to their final destination in another town. At this time the whole country was under curfew.

The sequel to this story is something Victor will always treasure. The driver was so touched by these events that Victor decided to share the gospel with him. The driver immediately accepted Jesus. 'This was our very first convert in that land,' Victor told me. 'And he's now studying at a Bible college!'

Conclusion

The leaders at KT do not want to develop a megachurch just to make it the biggest. This is a city church. And governments are more likely to take notice of what's happening among the populace when large crowds assemble. If it is merely a handful of Pentecostalists above a fish 'n chip shop in an obscure town, or a handful of Baptists somewhere else, they are not going to take much notice.

Already KT is attracting attention in high places since it began to fill some of the largest auditoriums in London, especially as it has done this without the support of other churches. The buildings KT uses are some of the largest in London, such as the Royal Albert Hall, Wembley Arena and London Arena. These events often attract the interest of the media and come to the notice of officials in government. 'I should make it clear that we are not thinking of an exclusive presence to the point of saying we are *the* church in London,' says Colin. 'We are standing with other people who are also thinking of London as a whole.' KT's vision is to see the answer to the last prayer of Jesus when he expressed his desire for the unity of all believers. It should mean that people will be able to merely walk across the street, or down their own road, and find a local church that will meet their needs locally. These local churches can then be networked into a city-wide vision.

So with a Christian presence which is linked up with a city-wide vision a good numerical goal will be achieved. For this to happen the central church must grow to at least 30,000 supplemented by 2,000 satellite churches within the orbit of the M25. These satellites would not be separate self-existent entities unconnected to the main body. The vision is not to do separate things in little corners but for them to be unified with the main church at the centre.

How can this be made to operate effectively? KT has already proved that the technology is available today with its satellite broadcasts. This enables KT to reach people across vast distances. This is not restricted to the current domestic television and radio stations who offer merely crumbs of communication facilities to evangelicals. KT is already using these communication tools via satellite dishes not only to sites in the London area, but across Europe. By this means the London City Church will be able to spread its influence beyond London. Colin's vision also takes him on a global mission. Last year he was in Brazil for the 'March for Jesus' rally and was able to speak to KT and its network in London. The stronger KT is here in London the greater will be its influence in the capital cities of the world. Some people are fearful of developments in the European Union, but when they come, KT plans to be ready to spread the message of the gospel of Jesus using all the 'high-tech' means at its disposal.

At governmental level, the Temple already has specific members of staff who are assigned to reach out into parliament. Lyndon Bowring and his staff are of considerable value. Members of Parliament also testify to the value of the London City Church.

Another significant feature of KT is the multi-cultural nature of its ministry. It shows that it is possible for people from a variety of ethnic backgrounds to work in harmony with each other.

In the preceding pages I have tried to give you the story of Kensington Temple. It's a personal story because I was there at the beginning of its modern development, with Eldin Corsic. Then I returned many years later to witness the ministries of Wynne Lewis and Colin Dye.

I believe that today's spiritual harvest is at root the result of the agonising prayers of Kensington's Christians 150 years ago. Consider these words of the psalmist: 'Those who plant in tears will harvest in shouts of joy. They weep as they go to plant their seed, but they sing as they return with the harvest' (Ps 126:5, 6, NLT). How closely this compares with this newspaper report of 1848: 'The members of Kensington's Hornton Street Congregational Church . . . had been deeply moved at a recent prayer meeting and many wept as they commissioned thirty-seven people who were to pioneer the work in Notting Hill.'

APPENDIX 1
Richard's Prophetic Song
These are the days of the latter rain
(Not by might)

These are the days of the latter rain
the Lord is pouring out His Spirit on the earth.
The devil trembles for he knows his time is short
soon the Lord will come with clouds of heaven.
Not by might, not by power but by my Spirit says the Lord
by my Spirit says the Lord not by might nor by power
but by my Spirit says the Lord.
We are building a city church, we are building a city church
with our God.
His end-time people, we are rising up to preach the gospel
and to spread the pow'r of good.
The Lord has promised.
He will build a mighty church and the gates of hell cannot
stand against us.

APPENDIX 2
The 10°40° Window

The 10°40° window on the world map represents the countries of Africa and Asia. It stretches from West Africa through the Middle East to the Far Eastern countries of Asia, where most of the people who have not heard of Christ and his message are to be found.

There are sixty-two countries in this window with 100 'gateway cities'. These 'gateways' open up avenues to the places where the 'unreached' live. In many of these countries there are pockets of indigenous peoples with no known missionaries, or Christians.

Peter Wagner says, 'The central, most powerful weapon of spiritual warfare is prayer . . . We must do whatever it takes to motivate and mobilise God's people everywhere for massive, prevailing, powerful and effective prayer for the lost . . . God is raising up praying people across geographic, denominational, racial and generational lines.' (Patrick Johnstone et al, eds, *The Unreached Peoples* [YWAM Publishing: ISBN 0 927545 98 5].)